A Banker Reflects on

Money, Love and Virtue

Maria José Pereira

Published in this first edition in 2015 by:
Triarchy Press
Station Offices
Axminster
Devon
EX13 5PF
England

+44 (0)1297 631456
info@triarchypress.net
www.triarchypress.net

A catalogue record for this book is available from the British Library.

Paperback ISBN: 978-1-909470-60-6
ePub ISBN: 978-1-909470-61-3
pdf ISBN: 978-1-909470-62-0

In memory of my husband,
Ernesto Melo Antunes,
and dedicated to the young
who will create the future.

Contents

Acknowledgements

I begin by thanking Graham Leicester, who accompanied me throughout the gestation of this book, the idea for which arose from a discussion, my first with him in September 2010, and culminated in his finding my editor and publisher. I am also grateful to other friends at International Futures Forum (IFF). In particular, I thank Napier Collyns, who prodded me along with valuable suggestions and encouraged me more than any other; Mick Costigan, who added to the content and form of my book with his structured and incisive thinking; Roberto Carneiro, who guided and supported me and introduced me to IFF; Maureen O'Hara, who helped with her critical reading of early writings; Andrew Lyon and Alison Linyard who allowed me the space to present and discuss my ideas at a seminar in Glasgow in October 2013; Tony Hodgson, Bill Sharpe and others who advised through a critical review of my manuscript at the Boathouse in the same month; and Martin Albrow, David Hodgson, David Lorimer, Jennifer Williams and Saul Wainwright for early contributions and discussion. I also thank Mairi Heneghan for the help she extended.

To Luigino Bruni, I give special thanks. Our weekly discussions over three months at the Sophia University Institute near Florence in 2011 allowed me greater insight into the writings of Aristotle, Adam Smith, Antonio Genovesi, John Stuart Mill and other economists. He enriched my understanding of the purpose of economics and how it need not be abstract but humane, with a place for virtue and friendship. I thank Piero Coda for a better understanding of Augustinian writings on love and I thank Antonio Baggio, Bennie Caillebaut, Benedetto Gui, Pier Luigi Porta, Judy Povlius and Sergio Rodinara for the opportunity to learn from these scholars. I am grateful to the economist Stefano Zamagni for receiving me at the University of Bologna. I was inspired by my conversations with him and by his wealth of knowledge, not only of economics but of history and civil society. I thank him also for generously reading, and suggesting improvements to chapters in this book.

I am grateful to Manuela Silva for her clarity of vision and intelligent expression and coherent example of 'a life well lived', and for her constant support and tireless critiques. I thank Peter Sprinkart for his professorial advice on my writings and for deepening conversation and friendship of many years. I thank João Lobo Antunes, neurosurgeon and writer, for generously critiquing my chapter on compassion and collaboration. I am grateful to my step-daughter, Joana Melo Antunes, whose perceptive reading gave the book a clearer voice. I thank my god-child, Charlotte Munson, and my niece, Amanda d'Almeida, who read drafts from the perspective of the younger audience that I hope to engage.

Old friends and ex-colleagues on Wall Street provided me with an avenue to discuss financial developments. They critiqued chapters on economics and finance. For this I thank Charles Abrecht, Charles Blood, Tom Hardy, Jonathan Hirst, Peter Munson, David Cripps and in particular Jeff Schoenfeld, Paul Drexler and Janet Nicolini for their presence and advice as I reworked my book. I am grateful to Paul Woolley for reinforcing my belief in investment with a long-term view and to John Fullerton for his commitment to constructive finance and natural capital. To other friends, for conversations and helpful criticism, I offer thanks: Richard and Marilyn Collier, Hilde Munson, Marianne Felici, Blake Lannon, Clare Micuda, John Lombardi, Zibby Munson, Fiona Walker, Herbie Weiss, Joan Wallace, Olivia Bina, Anne Cripps, Nora Lam, Flora Lam, Sweeta Motwani, Firoz Manji, Minnie Freudenthal and Manuel Rosário. And I remember Dinky Salzborn, my first reader, whom I miss in this world.

I thank Laurence Freeman, OSB, for the gift of meditation through the eye of the heart, which enables a deeper understanding of the world, and for teaching me that meditation is a first step towards action. I thank my cousins, Arthur and Barbara Leyden, for advising me on the cover design and for opening up their home as a base for my periods of study at the Cambridge Library, and my sister and her husband, Virginia and Carlos d'Almeida, for welcoming me and enabling my research in California. I thank Anca Ellenbroek for her kind hospitality in Italy and Monique Bryers for hers in London, so facilitating my research at the British Library. I thank relatives and friends for their support and understanding over my frequent 'disappearances' while working on my project. Although work on this book has taken four years, it is the result of the experience of a life, particularly with my husband, Ernesto Melo Antunes, who deepened my understanding of the Ciceronian ideal of the philosopher-statesman. I am grateful to my family, friends and people that I have encountered who convince me that the vision of money, love and virtue, working in harmony, is possible. I need not name them all; they will recognize themselves in these words.

I end by thanking my editor and publisher, Andrew Carey, for believing in my work and making my text clearer and more engaging. To all I am grateful for their contribution and take sole responsibility for my conclusion.

Preface

This book is a reflection on how money, love and virtue are intertwined. It is designed to be read by people who may not have an extensive knowledge of economics or finance, history or philosophy, but who have an interest in the present and the future. My intention is to engage again with the humanistic insights of great thinkers, some of whom we may have forgotten or overlooked, to help us to focus on our humanity, as the foundation for an economic and financial order that can serve us well. I look at a number of issues central to this discussion in order to illustrate how we are interlinked with our past and the present and with each other and how we define our present through action.

In our world, where economic and financial challenges appear to be increasingly overshadowed by threats to our peace and security, and where fear, antagonism and a loss of hope seem to have gripped many, it becomes more urgent that we be guided by an *imagined ideal*. More than ever, we need to reflect on what it means to be human and to collaborate in constructing a world where money, love and virtue work together and not in contradiction, for only in such a world can we find peace. I hope this book will prompt reflection, discussion and beneficial action, for together we form society and define the world in which we live.

Maria José Pereira (a.k.a. Melo Antunes)
1st March, 2015

Introduction

Reflection on Three Central Concepts

"We have involved ourselves in a colossal muddle,
having blundered in the control of a delicate machine,
the working of which we do not understand."
John Maynard Keynes

"History is always being begun anew; it is always working itself out."
Fernand Braudel

"The great secret of morals is love."
Percy Bysshe Shelley

The Path to Reflection
The Need for Reflection
Three Central Concepts
Design and Progression of the Book

The Path to Reflection

When money, love and virtue are mentioned in the same breath, most people respond with surprise and scepticism. What do these notions have in common? Surely they belong to different realms? Money and virtue? Mutually exclusive. Virtue is an old-fashioned ideal, with a hint of hypocrisy. Love? A romantic illusion. It has nothing to do with money, other than the love of it. Money is about competition and accumulation. So goes the typical response. But others are intrigued by the apparent contradiction and want to take the discussion further.

For myself, I have come to believe that money, love and virtue are not alien, nor even opposed, to one another, but intertwined. They thrive together. Representing different dimensions in our lives, they share a common ground in us, the people who live those lives. Money permits our material welfare and wellbeing. Love fulfils our emotional and spiritual needs. And love inspires virtue, which allows the person to live in harmony with the world. When all three are reconciled in a life, there is the seed of happiness. Where they are not, fragmentation, contradiction and opposition result – conditions that promote discontent. Once reconciled, money, love and virtue lead to a life well lived, a happy life, and permit a world of which many only dream.

How did I start this reflection? Having spent my whole career in finance, I observed with deep discomfort the gradual degeneration of the established financial model: the eruption of corporate scandals, such as WorldCom and Enron, the increase in leverage and speculation causing the collapse of Long-Term Capital Management,[1] and the eventual explosion of the subprime crisis leading to major financial disruption in 2008. The unethical, speculative and extractive behaviour that all this revealed was disconcerting. This kind of behaviour was becoming accepted and tolerated and in fact proliferating. The erosion and abuse of trust that permitted it took place largely unnoticed until the financial crisis finally and fully revealed it in all its dismal reality.

Reflecting on the financial malaise led me to ponder the purpose of money and to imagine a financial model that would better serve investors and the world at large. This led me initially to an inquiry into sustainable investment, a long-term approach that considers not only profits but also benefits to society and the preservation of nature. Sustainable investment integrates previously unmeasured components into the business model: environmental externalities and social factors.

While recognizing the urgent need to account for the depletion of nature and the effects of climate change – and the cost of redressing both – as well as incorporating social considerations into economic and business decisions, and in fact believing that the vision for sustainable investment is an exciting one, I became convinced that the issue confronting us was bigger than numbers alone could convey and that a purely market response was inadequate. There was something much deeper at play, something that touches our human condition, and that we can only address by reintegrating the human dimension into the financial and investment equation.

When, not yet confident of my own vision, I began discussing sustainable investment with other financial professionals, I vaguely conceded that investment is about making money, about self-interest[2] and not about morality. The financial collapse in 2008, followed by successive financial scandals and even fraud, revealed the inadequacy of this position and the myopic perception of self-interest that had been adopted. The crisis arising from the unfettered operation of financial markets due to the dismantling of regulation and laxity in supervision led to calls for the return of prudential regulation. While proper legislation clearly has a vital place, I sensed that alone it would not resolve the fundamental problem, for investment encompasses much more than making money at any price. It also entails responsibility to the community at large, which is implied by the idea of 'enlightened self-interest'. Economic wellbeing stems not simply from money creation, but also from ensuring the dignity of the human being who is at the heart of the economy.

The financial collapse spurred on attempts already under way to reform our economic model. Initiatives to address this challenge have included looking beyond economic growth into wellbeing and happiness. However, this approach depends largely on measurement using surveys and indicators. Is this an adequate way to deal with the reality of the human condition, or do we need to go beyond numbers? In conversation with an economist tasked with looking into wellbeing, including happiness, I asked why there is no discussion of philosophy within economics, for philosophy considers fundamental issues around happiness. His response was categorical: philosophy is subjective and economics is an objective science. Again I found myself in uncomfortable territory.

I needed to digest his comment, which is one that underpins our current view of economics and embarked on an exploration of philosophy and economics. After all, did not economics begin within the school of philosophy?[3] As money is central to economics, I felt a need to understand the purpose of money and its impact on human beings, to explore the role of debt and investment, and to analyse the degeneration of our financial system in recent times. I believed that in order to move forward, I had first to go back to classical thought to understand the rationale and philosophy inherent in the organization of society, to discover the original intentions and vision for the economy and money and to rediscover lessons offered throughout the course of history.

I also had to reflect on human behaviour and aspirations. I needed to reconcile the criticism rightly directed at the banking and investment world with the responsible behaviour of many bankers and investors that I know and esteem. I felt the crisis arose not from just one sector, but out of a disintegration of the fabric of society – a disintegration in which we all play a part. This disintegration contributed to all kinds of excesses, particularly in relation to money. For this reason, I believed it necessary to examine more than just the economy and finance. In my circle are to be found the privileged, others living their daily existence as best they can, as well as innocent victims of the financial collapse, angered by the consequences they, their family or country have had to suffer. All of them live within the same economic and financial system that has been created over time. Despite differences in material circumstances, all of them possess a similar desire for security, comfort, peace and happiness. Some have been helped by fate, others not.

In order to understand how our lives and our world are shaped and how this might be reflected in our economic and financial systems, I turned to a number of leading thinkers from classical Greece to the present day. In my study, both within the material and the personal realms, I discovered that important ideas associated with thinkers and writers of the past have often been partially (mis)represented or else interpreted and highlighted so as to appear to endorse a particular approach or point of view. Inconvenient gems that have been forgotten need to be recovered. When a message of hope has been left aside, it must be restored. So I shall refer to a wide range of writers from different disciplines: conservative as well as forward thinking, religious and not. Some may seem outdated or inconsequential. Some are in the news now. In this process it is impossible to include everyone of relevance, and I have certainly bypassed writers who are just as important as those mentioned. The ones I discuss are those whose words have struck me for their pertinence or timelessness. I pretend no expertise. But these writers helped me think, and perhaps they will do the same for you.

The Need for Reflection

This book is a reflection, which is an indispensable step towards the kind of understanding that leads to deeper knowledge. A lasting solution to any challenge cannot be arrived at without comprehending all its facets, and this important step goes beyond the gathering of information. Our society gives priority to information and logic. We prize data, statistics, modelling and theory. This is the objective world within which economics and science operate, giving us much that is essential. However, it is through the subjective world that we gain deeper understanding via experience and reflection.

In order to reflect, we need leisure or time that is not packed with activity. Leisure is often thought of as time for entertainment, but it can be time for thought, for reflection. That is why the German philosopher Joseph Pieper, in his essay on *Leisure: the Basis of Culture*, writes about 'intellectual contemplation'. Borrowing from Thomas Aquinas (1225-1274), Pieper argues that knowledge requires "an element of pure, receptive contemplation, or as Heraclitus says, of 'listening to the essence of things'".[4] It requires attention and penetrating thought.

He describes how great medieval scholastic thinkers drew a distinction between *ratio* or logic, and *intellectus* or contemplation. "*Ratio* is the power of discursive, logical thought, of searching and examination, of abstraction, of definition and drawing conclusions. *Intellectus,* on the other hand, is the name for the understanding... to which truth offers itself like a landscape to the eye."[5] It is getting a glimpse into universal truth and understanding what it is to be human. It is pure contemplation, without any discursive interaction. Today many call it meditation. In classical times and during the Middle Ages, no knowledge was seen to be complete without both reason and contemplation, the objective and the subjective.

In our times, we value *ratio*, but do not much appreciate *intellectus*. With the advent of Modernity we began to lose this very important dimension, as we focused primarily on objective science. There is no denying the advances that science has allowed us. It has indeed permitted us to enhance our living conditions through improved health and material welfare. It has opened up new horizons, including technology that can serve us, if used well. But in the process, it risks turning us into mechanical beings, who use our discoveries to our own detriment, by losing sight of the timeless wisdom gathered in the course of our civilization and forgetting our human dimension. In order to regain an appreciation of what it means to be human, I believe that we need to recover *intellectus*. Reflection is an indispensable part of any action that serves humanity, for it deepens knowledge and helps us to understand that action has ramifications that radiate out into the world.

Three Central Concepts

This book, a product of my own reflection, proposes that we explore an *imagined ideal* that will restore humanism, a dignified vision of life that has the relational aspect of our lives at its heart. For some people, humanism implies an agnostic view of life. This is not necessarily the case. Regardless of whether one subscribes to a religion or not, humanism presupposes consideration for the other, an intention to aim for the greater and common good and not simply for individual welfare. It involves living in harmony with each other and with nature.

Deep understanding and imagination are indispensable if we are to create a new reality with money, love and virtue working in beneficial union. At the most basic level, we organize ourselves around material achievement. Everyone understands this. Human action is prompted by material needs and they drive government policy. 'Basic needs' are for things indispensable to our survival, while 'surplus needs' bring comfort and pleasure. Hence, money,[6] which provides for material needs, is central to our wellbeing and allows us to flourish.

But there is another side to money, the nefarious side, which the recent international financial crisis unveiled. Developments leading up to that crisis are discussed later and serve as backdrop for the reflection of this book. The unrestrained pursuit of money creates harmful disruption, turning an indispensable and beneficial component of our economic system, money, into something destructive. In trying to understand the contradictions inherent in money, we shall explore the purpose of money, consider its two facets and see how the nefarious side may be tamed. That requires virtue.

Virtue makes the beneficial use of money possible. I use the word *virtue*, rather than ethics or responsibility, to highlight the Aristotelian concept of a life well lived. Aristotle is the starting point for this discussion. Not only was he a father of Western civilization, but he developed our thinking about money, love and virtue. He sees the economy as management of the material needs of the *polis,* or city state, and money as the unit of exchange for goods and services in the marketplace. For citizens to be well served in the *polis*, the use of money must be beneficial. Aristotle believes that in order to achieve this, a central requirement is proportionality, the appropriate division of wealth and resources. He writes not of equality, but proportionality, which is governed by justice, the central virtue.

How is virtue possible? For Aristotle, virtue is enabled by *philia* or friendship, which the Greeks represented as "the crown of life and the school of virtue".[7] *Philia* is love, inspiring virtue that ensures the smooth functioning of the *polis,* thereby permitting human flourishing, a precondition of *eudaimonia* or happiness:[8] "everyone enjoys as much happiness as he possesses virtue and wisdom, and acts according to their dictates".[9] Through friendship or love, virtue is made possible, and through virtue human flourishing and happiness arise, further expanding love.

In our times, we often talk about compassion, which is to partake of another's suffering. Love is born in compassion, but goes beyond it. Love results in joy, through which it replenishes itself, making love an infinite resource. It cannot flourish in isolation; participation is required. We do not discuss love as the fulfilment of a fleeting desire or as possession leading to pleasure. Rather, love is that which unifies, which defines us as human and which permits harmony and happiness. Understanding the potential of love, within our intricate interlinkages, is vital to any solution to the challenges we face. For many contemporary thinkers, love is a central theme of the new anthropology. Humanism can blossom with love.

Some may ask how we can reconcile love and money, as one deals with the ethereal and the other the material. But we can view both as satisfying different facets of the person. We cannot flourish if either is missing; both sustain us. If we arrive at understanding the connection between love and money, via consideration for the other and the common good, we will be able to grasp what it means to restore humanism to the economy and to finance. A vital component allowing for this is virtue. With reciprocity, love given and received, the practice of virtue is possible; without love, it is difficult.

Is such a vision realistic? Most may see this as an unattainable ideal. However, I maintain that we should not discard an ideal, simply because it seems unattainable. We can use it as a beacon to guide us. People like Martin Luther King, Mahatma Gandhi, Nelson Mandela and, in our contemporary world, the Dalai Lama and Pope Francis, with their elevated vision of humanity, have inspired many of us. If we desire a better world, we have to imagine a way and work towards it within society.[10] Our general perception of human nature is informed by a dark view, which is usually justified by reference to our history of aggression and violence, which we continue to live out today. This is seen as reality, but it encompasses just part of the human being and of our lives. Must we continue to entrap ourselves in a perception of reality based on unending strife and misery? Or, in shaping our social relations and our relationship with institutions and the state, can we evoke a more beneficial vision of humanity and steer our language and social norms towards a kinder future? Such a vision can be termed true or 'enlightened self-interest', for no self-interest that fails to consider the interests of the whole can provide lasting benefit.

These are important issues for concerned citizens to explore, reflect on, discuss and collaborate over, in order to create an economic and financial framework that will permit a more promising future. This is not a portrait of Utopia; rather it is a portrait of uncorrupted life,[11] for which there is deep yearning. I do not suggest that perfection can be arrived at, but if the influence of good is increased, so will outcomes be improved. Reflection and responsible action are indispensable and involve all, for "we are society".[12] Let us explore a solution through love and virtue, acting within the material realm of money to ensure that money serves its purpose. It is an *ideal* worth striving for, and along with many others, I believe that it is essential for our future and for our survival.

Design and Progression of the Book

This book is designed for people with an interest in the economic and financial system and how it may better serve the human community, even if the ramifications of the discussion go beyond that. My study of the material organization of society has helped me to realize that in order for people to be served with dignity, we must also live in dignity. This book offers a way to bring discussion of the immaterial into the realm of the material and to emphasize the importance of individual and collective action. Together we constitute society and shape our world.

The chapters that follow are connected essays dealing with key themes in our exploration. They portray my own reading. They are not intended to present an in-depth study of the issues, but to encourage deeper thinking about them. My purpose is to provoke reflection on important interlinkages, as a first step hopefully in bringing about understanding and beneficial action. In collaboration, we can move forward towards a better world. We are in crisis. We must *imagine* a better future and work towards it.

Chapter 1 looks at the economy as the process of managing our material needs, and money as the unit of exchange within the marketplace. It examines how the introduction of credit advanced human welfare by allowing trade and economies to expand and cities to flourish. Money has played a vital role in liberating humans from dependence, thereby explaining the strong association between money and our ideas of liberty. Investment helps build the future.

Chapter 2 examines how the process of 'financialization', while contributing to a virtuous cycle in its early phase, saw toxic elements creep in. Investment has assumed characteristics far removed from those it originally displayed, as a focus on the short term has become increasingly prevalent. While constructive finance allows enhanced economic welfare and progress, finance has shown its dark side through high leverage, a focus on short-term trading, speculation, excessive extraction of income, and even fraud, aided by deregulation and deficient supervision. The current financial model has contributed to inequality, a central challenge today, and to the destruction of our financial commons. It needs to be put right. Financial reform has begun with the introduction of regulation and more stringent capital requirements, but full reform cannot be accomplished unless this is accompanied by a reform of the behaviour of those acting within the financial system, by their fully considering the consequences of their action.

Chapter 3 discusses how the economy, when treated as an abstract concept without giving full consideration to the human beings it is designed to serve, can undo material improvements and dehumanize society, causing discontent. How we view *self-interest* and how we treat nature will influence our wellbeing. Consumption is not the purpose of life, and waste contributes to environmental degradation. The use and development of technology has implications for our humanity. While our renewed interest in the idea of happiness aims to restore the human dimension, it is not sufficient simply to provide new aggregate measures of happiness within our economic models. For true progress, we need to fully appreciate and restore the human dimension.

Chapter 4 examines the influence that our assumptions about human nature have on our actions. A negative and pessimistic view has not served us well. I suggest we reinstate a presumption of the underlying virtue of humanity with a perspective that embraces consideration and respect for the person and concern for the *common good*. In this way we will be able to restore virtue and dignity to the market. Justice comprises perfect law and institutions and also good action. Liberty entails a regard for the other through respect for the other's liberty. Virtue is served by understanding our human connection, relationship and interdependence.

Chapter 5 looks at compassion, which enables virtue. Biologists observe that evolution has resulted in greater cooperation and even altruism in some cases. Neuroscientists confirm the human capacity for empathy, which allows for the elaboration of moral rules, laws and justice systems. Through collaboration, we ensure that human needs are properly met within the economy and finance. True or *enlightened self-interest* must encompass the other and the universe at large.

Chapter 6 discusses love, which is our essence. Love is transcendental, but it is also human. It allows us to see the other in ourselves and to realize our full potential. It is the only resource that is infinite, as it replenishes itself through the joy it unleashes. Justice is the uniting of power and love. Love leads to unity and harmony, to a life well lived. It is the deepest manifestation of humanity and of happiness.

The **Integration** draws together all these threads. Finance should be a tool to realize human advancement. It is a means to provide investment, innovation, growth and prosperity. It requires trust and civic action, enabled by virtue. Love, incorporating respect, true understanding and collaboration, makes virtue possible. When working in harmony, money, love and virtue realize our social contract, a foundation of civilization. In this way a humanistic world can blossom and contribute to the common good.

Part I: The Material: Money

Chapter 1

The Economy and Money: Original Purpose

"Economics is merely the study of mankind in the ordinary business of life."
Alfred Marshall

"Economics... is not an exact science; it is in fact, or ought to be, something much greater; a branch of wisdom."
E.F. Schumacher

"Another name for debt is credit, a word derived from the Latin 'credere,' to believe. When we borrow or lend money, it is an act both of trust and of confidence."
Philip Coggan

The Economy: Managing Material Needs
The Market: a Place of Beneficial Exchange
Money: the Life-Blood of Society
Banking and Credit: Money Creation
Expanding Liberty and Prosperity
Investing in the Future
Restating the Human Purpose

~~~

Money facilitates market exchange and ensures the flow of goods and services; without money, the economy cannot function smoothly. Credit and investment permit economic flourishing and long-term wealth creation; investment builds the future. With the coming of Modernity, economic activity came to be seen as offering a chance for prosperity, enabling equality and ensuring liberty, as in the vision espoused by Adam Smith. This continues to be the key ideology underpinning free markets and competition, linking our economic aspirations with our political vision. However, the economic outcome depends on human action.

~~~

The Economy: Managing Material Needs

In his 'Treatise on Government', *The Politics,* Aristotle (384-322 BCE) begins with the declaration: "We see that every city is a society, and every society is established for some good purpose". He continues: a "society of many families [is] instituted for their lasting, mutual advantage".[1] Indeed, each household within society must organize its material requirements, those things that are indispensable for existence. The management of these needs is referred to as *oikos-nomos*, which denotes the 'law of the home' or 'home governance' in Greek. Thus, within each family unit, the 'ideal' economy was designed as a means of satisfying the family's requirements, with every member playing a vital role. The economy continues to be of utmost importance in the management of material needs today.

In Aristotle's time, the household comprised the master of the estate, his family and slaves. Some may think that Aristotle's vision is not appropriate for discussion here, because of its autocratic organization and the fact that his *polis* or city state, with slaves and women in subjugation, was quite different from our free and expanded world economy today. However, I believe it worth examining in order to understand the key objectives underlying an economy and the means by which they were attained in Aristotle's time, for this helps us to know its purpose, as well as the role of money and the impact of human behaviour.

Aristotle writes that it is part of human nature to require food, the most basic of needs. For him, the economy has a boundary, for it is to provide what we need. It is not limitless: "the acquisition of those possessions which are necessary for a happy life is not infinite". Within the economy, the family must manage properly what it needs. As human organization expanded into villages and then cities, families could no longer remain self-sufficient, so barter or exchange came into being. Within Aristotle's 'ideal' economy, production was the first step, for without production there were no goods. Excess goods, unnecessary for domestic use, were sold so as to acquire other goods that were either needed or preferred. Money was introduced in order to facilitate exchange, and the marketplace began to play a key role. In trade, a good or commodity is exchanged for money, which, in turn, is exchanged for another good or commodity.

For Aristotle, acquiring something by trade for use is legitimate; it has necessary value. Acquisition for pure monetary gain, or chrematistics, is not. Aristotle differentiates between *needs* and *wants.* For him needs are natural, and while an "economy requires the possession of wealth, [it is] not on its own account but with another view, to purchase things necessary therewith". Hence, he sees "money-making" for the "breeding of money" as "censurable", a dehumanizing activity. In our complex world, trade and gain are viewed through different prisms, and trade has helped advance human welfare. The accumulation of money or pure monetary gain is a fundamental characteristic of modern economics and finance, within the capitalist system. By studying Aristotle, however, we can perhaps see how money or property can be used well. After all, Aristotle also writes that "property is as an instrument to living". It plays a fundamental role.

His primary goal for the *polis* is harmony, a precondition for happiness. Harmony is made possible by the smooth functioning of the economy, thereby ensuring the common good. Each family contributed to the economic ideal, as described in *The Politics*. Just as in a household, today in our economy each member can play their part to ensure its proper functioning. Our global stage is much larger and more populous than in classical times. We live in a world with billions of households and multiple states and cultures. Most people have more rights than in Aristotle's hierarchical times, when women and serfs were not considered citizens. And the economic reality today is more complex and intricate. Nonetheless, we must understand the underlying objectives of the economy, if it is to work effectively, and each member of society must play his requisite part towards this end.

Our economic sophistication is advanced, but the underlying purpose for which the economy is organized remains the same: to meet the material needs of every member of society. It is designed firstly to respond to our most basic requirements, what we need in order to exist: food, shelter, clothing, health and other physical necessities. It ensures our safety and, in an affluent society, it provides leisure, art and luxuries, which give pleasure. Indeed, the economy is effectively the management of the provision of material things. With proper management, humans flourish. Equally, our wellbeing can be disturbed, either through denial of our material needs or through dissonance and discord caused by malfunctions of the economic system, such as extreme disparity in wealth and financial abuse.

Aristotle writes that humans are social and have "a perception of good and evil, of just and unjust, and it is a participation of these common sentiments which forms a family and a city". For him, justice benefits all and implies proportionality, an appropriate sharing of resources, and he warns against the dangers arising from encroachment by the rich. Thus, for Aristotle the central requirement underpinning a well-functioning city is proportionality enabled by justice, which he describes as the virtue most necessary to society[2] and the one that renders possible all other virtues. Justice safeguards democracy and peace and holds in check vices like avarice, fraud and deceit.

This premise remains unchanged today. We prefer to use the term 'responsibility' or 'ethics', rather than 'virtue', but nonetheless, this represents the same idea and encapsulates key characteristics for a well-functioning society, such as trust and justice. If we analyse each of these traits, we realize that none of them is possible without other underlying values. For example, trust is made possible by honesty and transparency, and justice by sympathy, temperance and self-restraint. Law alone cannot guarantee the realization of justice. A regard for other people is vital, and this leads to responsible action. The Greeks referred to this holistic approach to wellbeing for the *polis* as simply 'virtue', and this is why I choose to use this term throughout the book. Virtue is a foundation for a well-functioning society and economy, because it governs beneficial human behaviour and makes possible a harmonious outcome.

The Market: A Place of Beneficial Exchange

The market is where the exchange of goods and services occurs. Aristotle believes fairness or proportionality of exchange to be vital in markets. In the *Nichomachean Ethics* he discusses the proper ratio for exchanging property, a ratio that is just and required for harmony, the ideal for the Greek *polis.* Such behaviour is governed by virtue: "that city is happiest which is the best and acts best, for no one can do well who acts not well".[3] A person possessing virtue knows what action is appropriate or just. Aristotle believes this condition stems from *philia* (friendship) and ensures *eudaimonia* (happiness or human flourishing). It remains true today that reciprocity, or mutual assistance founded on friendship and collaboration, helps ensure a beneficial market and proportional exchange that builds community.

Proportional exchange need not be fully equal, but it must be seen to be appropriate, to be just.[4] Aristotle writes of "good morals and a system of equal laws"[5] in this regard. Most of us have witnessed social conflict that arises when one party feels abused and believes that he is not getting his proper due. This can lead to anger and violence, causing conflict and jeopardizing harmony. In *The Politics*, Aristotle writes about the risk of revolution and sedition arising from injustice. Excessive encroachment, due to greed, goes against the principle of proportionality and is seen as an affront to justice. Aristotle and his teacher, Plato, presented greed as a social rather than an individual problem. Greed is a major problem in our society today. It can be motivated by a fear of shortage in the future, leading to hoarding. It can stem from avarice, the desire to consume more, or pride, the desire to appear better off than one really is. Thomas Aquinas, who reinterprets Aristotle within Christian thinking, likewise sees legitimacy in any exchange designed to meet a need, but condemns avarice: "the desire for gain, which knows no bounds but spreads always further".[6]

The contemporary economists Luigino Bruni and Robert Sugden write that if the market is to be beneficial, it must maintain relations of mutual assistance (friendship) and distribution of gains must not deviate too far from standards of fairness (justice).[7] In a beneficial market, each agent is free to determine what contract to enter into and each is symmetrically positioned with respect to a mutually useful relationship, in contrast to an asymmetric relationship of advantaged and disadvantaged.[8] Thus, they argue that markets can support liberty (freedom to enter into a contract) and equality (symmetric relationships), as well as virtuous behaviour (fair and beneficial exchange). Markets function best when they are underpinned by trust in a fair exchange, where each transaction provides benefits to everyone who is a party to it. Although individuals act in their own interest, mutual benefit results.

Money: the Life-Blood of Society

In the marketplace, barter initially served as the method of exchange. Goods and services were traded for other goods and services. But due to unequal value in what was exchanged, barter was found to be inadequate and cumbersome. Money was then established as a unit of exchange to facilitate trade. The textbook definition of money is "a medium of exchange, means of unilateral payment or settlement, measure of value or unit of account and store of value".[9] A historian whose analysis of capitalism is highly regarded, Fernand Braudel, writes that "money is a very old invention... without exchange, there is no society".[10] Likewise, Geoffrey Ingham refers to it as "one of our essential social technologies... a foundation of the world's first large-scale societies in the ancient Near East during the 3rd millennium BCE". In use for thousands of years, money has permitted trade to flourish and societies to develop, by facilitating the supply of necessary goods via exchange and thus allowing for improving standards of living.

Since money is able to store value as pure purchasing power, it allows for transactional flexibility. Ingham discusses how money allows transactions to be deferred, revised, reactivated or cancelled. Money has no time limit, no expiration date. In a market of exchange, the seller of a good need not accept another good in immediate return. With the money received, he can purchase another good in another market or at a later date. Money thus allows economic action to cover extensive territories and to be carried over from the past or projected into the future. John Kenneth Galbraith writes that most things are important only to those who have them, but money is important to all.[11] It is the unit through which the exchange of material things passes and it facilitates our welfare.

In medieval times, Franciscan monks were the first to compare money to blood in the body,[12] and in the 18th century François Quesnay, the economist and physician to Louis XV, extended this analysis. The economist John Maynard Keynes himself describes money as the "life-blood of industry".[13] And we can see money as the life-blood of society, since it brings the 'life force' to different parts of the economy. Just as an orderly flow of blood through the body ensures health, so does the way money flows within society determine its welfare. Without the flow of blood, the body dies; likewise, the economy atrophies without the flow of money. And just as blood can bring nutrients, it can also bring toxins. Thus, the health of the economy is governed by the beneficial flow of money.

Debates on the nature of money are as old as their subject. Galbraith questions whether the economy begins with production or with money creation and whether money influences the economy or responds to the economy. Aristotle would have said that the economy begins with production and money facilitates exchange. David Hume and classical economists referred to money as neutral, and Friedrich Hayek introduced the term 'neutral veil' to describe money.[14] These economists saw money as providing a neutral framework to permit economic activity. They believed that money does not itself determine outcome or create new value, but rather the use of money does. Hence, they saw any change in the stock of money as not affecting the underlying real variables, such as production, employment and consumption, but simply influencing price and wage levels. Ludwig von Mises, a friend of Hayek's, believed that money is never neutral. He postulated that it is a market phenomenon, demanded for its usefulness in buying goods and that credit expansion by banks causes business cycles, booms and bust.[15]

Keynes inverted the theory that money is neutral by introducing the monetary circuit or productive theory of money in his *Treatise on Money*: money as a creator of wealth. He argued that through central banking activity and bank lending, the creation of money is a starting point for economic activity and wealth creation. Thus, money is not neutral. Banks create money through a "monopoly of magic",[16] and the firm negotiates a loan and invests in productive activity, with people supplying labour. The financialization[17] of the economy has brought us one step beyond Keynes's vision. Our economy today is not defined by the creation of money simply for investment in productive assets and job-creation, but by the creation of money to a large extent for consumption and paper investment. In our current economic and financial paradigm, money is definitely seen to lead the economy.

Banking and Credit: Money Creation

Initially using commodities like beads and gold and then metal coins, money subsequently took on the form of paper or *fiat* money, backed by the promise to pay. This allowed for the development of banking. Laurence Fontaine notes that the word 'credit' stems from the Latin *credo* – 'I believe' – which is linked to *fides,* faith or confidence.[18] Hence, credit is founded on confidence that the money lent will be returned. In the English language, linked to the role of banking is the word 'fiduciary', the definition of which is "a person legally appointed and authorized to hold assets in trust for another person. The fiduciary manages the assets for the benefit of the other person rather than his or her own profit."[19] Within the banking system, the fiduciary is an agent, working for the client on the basis of trust. Trust is equally expected of the borrower. As originally conceived, credit is not a given. It has to be justified through confidence. As part of the money system, credit has to be properly guarded because, if it is abused, access to it can be lost. Indeed trust was intended to be the foundation for banking and credit, a fiduciary responsibility often forgotten today.

Within the Western world, banking originated in Italy. The creation of letters of credit[20] permitted the flourishing of trade in the 13th century in Genoa and was extended in the 14th century to Venice, where Rialto Square was the heart of all exchange. Development of the *commenda,* a rudimentary type of joint stock, issued separately for each trade mission and allowing those who financed the trade to participate in the profits, expanded trade further.[21] By 1500, the Arsenal in Venice comprised the largest industrial complex in the world. It was capable of building, arming, provisioning and launching eighty galleys at a speed and level of consistency unmatched by any rival.[22] This was the original germination of finance and globalization. A complex commercial society was made possible by credit and trade.

Franciscan monks were important to the development of finance in Italy, for within the order were merchant lay members who understood its role. In Venice in the late 15th century, Friar Luca Pacioli published the *Review of Arithmetic, Geometry, Ratio and Proportion,* adapted from mathematics developed in the Muslim world. He included the first printed treatise on book-keeping in the West, thus providing the foundation for modern accounting. Pacioli also devised company shares as a way to diversify risk, and to permit the raising of capital for trade and commerce and of public debt for government spending.[23] Importantly, amidst expanding economic activity, Franciscans reinforced the concept of the *common good* as the final objective of the economy. This is in line with the Aristotelian concept of flourishing in the *polis.*

In the medieval world, credit helped to tide over the less fortunate in difficult times, such as periods of exceptionally high expenses. Peasants had to resort to credit when crops were poor, to pay duties and to finance major family events such as marriage or death.[24] Since at that time borrowing arose mainly from hardship and heavy debt service entrapped many in poverty, interest was considered usury.[25] In response to the needs of the poor, Franciscan monks established the first *monte di pietà*, a form of credit institution, in Perugia in 1462.[26] The loans provided by the *montes* were funded by donations and did not bear interest. Later they were pledged by the borrowers' goods, as in pawning.

The argument for making loans rather than offering charity was that it allowed for the preservation of dignity, which begging did not. Moreover, it provided the opportunity for economic improvement when credit was used for agricultural or commercial purposes. Half a millennium later, Muhammad Yunus was similarly inspired to start Grameen Bank, so as to make credit available to the poor in Bangladesh at non-usurious rates.[27] He founded the bank with his own limited funds as established banks had refused any loan, on the grounds that the poor have 'no credit history'.

Montes proliferated and by the 16th century were no longer exclusively concerned with helping the poor. The further development of trade and commerce necessitated credit. Thomas Aquinas had unblocked the impediment to credit development that arose from the prohibition of interest or usury in the 13th century. He allowed for interest to be charged in commercial transactions via the *commenda*, provided the owner of the capital shared in the risk.[28] This was in line with the advocacy of economic freedom by the Scholastics, the academics of medieval universities in Europe who included Aquinas.[29] Banking expanded with the Medicis, who used the *montes* to finance trade and foreign politics, including war, during the Renaissance.

Banking was given further impetus by the monetary needs of war across Europe.[30] In the late 17th century when William of Orange sought funds to fight Louis XIV, William Patterson of Scotland suggested forming a banking company under royal charter. The full subscription of capital by the public was subsequently lent to William of Orange in the form of a note issue, which was backed by government guarantee. The Bank of England was thus created in 1694, firstly as a private bank and then subordinated to the Treasury in setting policy in 1931 and nationalized in 1946. In a similar vein, raising the capital needed to satisfy Napoleon's desire for conquest led to the foundation in 1800 of the Banque de France. In Germany in 1875, shortly after the establishment of the German Empire, the former Bank of Prussia became the Reichsbank, a precursor to the Central Bank, established in 1948.

Other than banks set up by states, private financial institutions were founded in order to make loans, thus facilitating the creation of money. In the early days of banking, monetary notes were backed by gold or other commodities. With the expansion of money, at different points in history, notes no longer had to be guaranteed by physical assets. Money was then created via a simple accounting entry, a 'promise to pay'.

The Bank of England's *Quarterly Bulletin* 2014 Q1[31] points to a common misconception that banks act simply as intermediaries, lending out deposits previously placed by savers. In fact, money is created by commercial banks making loans, which result in new bank deposits, the main form of money today.[32] Theoretically, banks are restricted in money creation through competition (governing profitable lending), prudential regulation and practice (such as that governing capital and reserves) and consumer action (households can *destroy* money by paying back loans). Management of risk, both credit and liquidity, should in theory constrain the banking system in money creation.[33] Monetary policy acts as the ultimate influence through interest rate policy (setting the price of reserves) in normal times and through quantitative easing (QE) under exceptional circumstances.[34] QE boosts the amount of money in circulation through the purchase of financial assets by the Central Bank, thus adding to the amount of bank deposits held by the seller of assets, the investor.

Easy money and lax controls can give rise to speculative bubbles and subsequent collapse and restructuring, of which there are many examples in history.[35] One such is the bubble arising from speculation in copper and leading to the collapse of the Knickerbocker Trust Bank of New York in 1907. This development led to calls for the creation of an agency that could ensure stability through proper supervision and policy and provide liquidity as the 'lender of last resort', thus helping prevent another crisis. Consequently, the Federal Reserve Act was passed in 1913 and the Federal Reserve Bank formed the following year. The US Congress established three key objectives for monetary policy in the Federal Reserve Act: maximum employment, stable prices and moderate long-term interest rates. It equipped the Federal Reserve Bank with two tools to prevent or moderate panic: the supervision and regulation of banks and the power to make loans to banks.[36]

The history of money is a long one and it is filled with stories of excess and collapse.[37] It is not my purpose here to examine it extensively but to discuss briefly the original concept of the economy and evolution of money, in order to understand the economic and financial framework and the role money plays. However, we can see that the original objective of both was to serve society by providing for economic welfare and advance and that confidence is an indispensable foundation of banking and finance. When trust is abused or squandered or when money is used in a destructive way, crisis follows. In recent times, we have witnessed the damage wrought by the abuse of money and a major breakdown of trust. So we see that banking and finance can be both creative and destructive.

Expanding Liberty and Prosperity

As well as enabling welfare by fulfilling our material needs, money – by allowing for the purchase of property – began increasingly to be seen as permitting liberty. Along with other liberal philosophers, John Locke (1632-1704) associates the owning of property with liberty: being "free from restraint and violence from others... [able] to dispose, and order, as he lists, his Person, Actions, Possessions, and his whole Property".[38] Locke justifies property rationally and ethically from the fundamental natural law of self-preservation, but he sees property also as a foundation for a social contract, to guard against "trespass against the whole Species". He sees property as giving continuity to a political society, joining generation to generation. For him, property acquisition cannot be unlimited, as it is "confined originally to what a man or his family could consume or use, and must not be wasted". In this respect, his view is similar to Aristotle's idea of an economic boundary and his ideal of proportionality.

Locke's theory of freedom is not simply absence of restraint; it is positive, for it is enlarged by the creation of society and government and laws. Government is of institution, of law. He writes that law makes humans free in the political arena, just as reason makes humans free in the universe. Locke maintains the right to revolt if the law is not upheld. Trust and contract are two pillars guaranteeing property and cohesive freedom within civil society. He calls for all to be "trusted with the means of maintaining the humanity of all *Community*". Citizenship implies formation of a 'living body' out of separate selves. For Locke, natural political virtue arises primarily because of symmetry; each possesses virtue that is other-regarding. There is a mutual consideration that involves all and that ensures the smooth functioning of society. Citizenship is a specific duty in a world where every individual either recognizes his responsibility for every other or disobeys his conscience. Freedom is accompanied by beneficial restraint. There is, therefore, an ethical element in Locke's theory as well as a principle of communal unity, accompanying the ideal of liberty.

Thomas Hobbes (1588-1679) by contrast defines liberty as "the absence of... external Impediments of motion"[39] to pursue self-interest, power and personal property. Hobbes lived through violent times including the Civil War in England, which helped him form a pessimistic view of humankind. In his book, *Leviathan,* which was written in the closing period of the war, Hobbes proposes a social contract, whereby one would voluntarily limit one's freedom of action and subject it to the state and to law, in order to gain protection from the greatest evil, that of violence. His view is based on fear and is defensive, while Locke's is based on hope and is expansive. One is built on a negative view of humans as violent and fearful, and the other on a positive view of humans as possessing conscience and being worthy of trust and capable of unity. In fact, Locke directed his *Two Treatises* against Hobbes,[40] whom he refused to meet. Both lived at a time when property or wealth became increasingly seen as a pre-condition of liberty. Today we continue to use this argument to justify the owning of property, and hence wealth, but we tend towards Hobbes's view of the human being, rather than Locke's. The latter's foundational treatment of trust and stewardship in property rights is not referred to as often as Hobbes's perspective of fear and the need for protection from violence and loss.

In the 18th century, the pursuit of liberty continued. The beginnings of Modernity and flowering of the Enlightenment saw a period of exciting intellectual ferment, political change and scientific progress. Economic acceleration accompanied great societal transformation. Cities swallowed village markets, with commerce replacing feudalism as the organizing force in society.[41] During this period, the wealth of the aristocracy was gradually supplanted by the new wealth of commercial agents. The market's importance as a place of trade and wealth-creation advanced. In this context, a new economic vision appeared that spoke to the needs of its time and that continues to underpin the economic theory of markets today. It arose from a critique by Adam Smith (1723-1790) of mercantilism, the prevailing theory of the time, which held that the world's wealth was fixed, with trade a zero-sum game.[42] High tariffs and restrictions on trade were the order of the day, in order to protect the wealth of those who had it and many wars were fought in Europe to defend special interests. Such strict controls over the economy were seen by Smith to limit freedom and not benefit the people, but rather to favour established merchants via state-sanctioned monopolies, and to benefit the state via taxes.

Adam Smith proposes in *The Wealth of Nations* a new economic synthesis, appealing to a world clamouring for liberty and equality and a chance to participate in prosperity. Smith writes: "It is not from the benevolence of the butcher, the brewer, or the baker, that we expect our dinner, but from their regard to their own interest.

We address ourselves, not to their humanity but to their self-love, and never talk to them of our own necessities but of their advantages. Nobody but a beggar chooses to depend chiefly upon the benevolence of his fellow-citizens."[43] He proposes beneficial competition, motivated not by benevolence but by self-interest, resulting in contribution to the public good via an 'invisible hand': "[the merchant] intends only his own gain, and he is in this, as in many other cases, led by an invisible hand to promote an end which was no part of his intention". Smith thus argues that each agent pursuing his self-interest contributes to the welfare of all. Not only did his vision permit material advancement, but also human progress, for it allowed men to cease being beggars and become free agents. The quest for liberty and the right to prosperity are very important considerations in explaining Smith's vision and its widespread adoption and underpin the important role it continues to play in the liberal order today.

Within the context of societal change, this was a powerful message, promising independence and a world of abundance. In 1776, the year Smith's book first appeared, the United States of America was founded, with Thomas Jefferson highlighting in the Declaration of Independence the "inalienable rights of life, liberty and the pursuit of happiness". Just over a decade later in 1789, the French Revolution was to proclaim "liberty, equality and fraternity". This was the *zeitgeist* or spirit of the times – liberty and equality – and Smith's economic model supported this vision. Without liberty and equality, all could not share in prosperity. Without prosperity, happiness is more difficult to attain.

Although in our days fraternity is less often associated with Adam Smith than are self-interest and competition, it is important to review his objectives. In line with Aristotle, Smith's vision is for the public good, via prosperity for all. For him, trade serves as a foundation for social harmony and the expansion of wealth.[44] He thought that the more privileged strata of society had a duty to ensure that everyone benefited from wealth expansion. His was a manifestation of fraternity, of sympathy or concern for the other, with a belief that this was essential for the common good. We also saw earlier the importance that Locke placed on regard for the other. This regard is governed by *conscience* in the case of Locke and by *self-command* in the case of Smith.[45]

The economist Mark Skousen notes that Adam Smith's classical self-regulating model leads to a natural harmony of interests through the invisible hand and involves three characteristics: freedom, competition and justice.[46] While the first two stem from self-interest, we can see that justice, which was also an important feature of commercial exchange for Aristotle, implies 'self-command'. Skousen highlights two hypotheses in Smith's synthesis: 1) a system of natural liberty leads to a higher standard of living, and 2) economic liberalism benefits rich and poor alike. Smith's approach has been adopted by neo-classicists and liberals in recent times to defend unfettered markets with quite different results, as income disparity widens. As a result, the assumption of 'trickle-down economics' via the invisible hand has been shown to be mistaken. Joseph Stiglitz explains that in our current economic system this has occurred because of a violation of fairness, or justice.[47] This is a key feature in Smith's self-regulating model, as underlined above. In liberal economics, the focus is on liberty, but justice or proportionality is ignored. Without justice, there is no self-regulation or self-command – both implicit in Smith's approach – and the invisible hand is rendered ineffective.

Adam Smith was firstly a moral philosopher. Seventeen years before *The Wealth of Nations*, he wrote *The Theory of Moral Sentiments*. The philosophical framework within which Smith lived and worked was that of moral sentiments, involving sympathy and incorporating propriety, justice, merit and duty.[48] It was an ethical framework with virtue playing an important part. He saw no conflict between self-interest and sympathy as self-interest was tempered by self-command; greed was restrained. Smith lived a modest life. His economic model was based on thrift and hard work and self-interest for him was enlightened; the key word is 'enlightened'. This implies wisdom, an understanding of the consequences of one's action and its ramifications for the society with which one is concerned. This requires self-command, which is expressed through virtue, in considering the consequences of one's actions. In this regard, Smith's thinking is similar to that of Aristotle and Locke. We have forgotten self-command in our current understanding of self-interest and the invisible hand.

Investing in the Future

From early times investment has been recognized as enabling economic development and the creation of wealth, and many economists have written about this. Adam Smith distinguished between 'circulating capital', used in trade to exchange one good for another and permitting immediate consumption, and 'fixed capital' used to generate an enhanced revenue or profit in future via an improvement in output. This occurs by the purchase of useful machines and instruments of trade, profitable buildings, the improvements of land, and education or apprenticeship.[49] For Smith, fixed capital is derived from and supported by circulating capital and obtained by deductions from the revenue of society, i.e. by saving.

Smith sees prodigality as hurtful as it increases the expense to society, because wasteful consumption impacts negatively on the establishment of a permanent fund for supporting investment. The 'permanent fund' enables investment which promotes industry and increases the amount of consumption by society over time. In his discussion, Smith refers to 'seed' as fixed capital, for "the farmer makes his profit not by its sale, but by its increase". Thus, investment is using saved funds to increase future revenues, just as planting of seeds causes crops to grow.

Our current view of money is quite different from that held in Smith's days. As Keynes writes, money can be created like "magic"[50] by banks booking loans. We focus today on consumption and financial trading rather than investment for the long term. Adam Smith's view of frugality is seen as outdated and rendered unnecessary by money creation via central banking and commercial banking activities, but the design of investment to enhance future welfare remains crucial and wastage of resources is equally pertinent today, especially in an environmentally challenged world.

Another economist, Jean-Baptiste Say (1767-1832), depicted the benefits of savings for economic growth.[51] He also saw saving as a stimulus to wealth creation, because it is used in the production of capital goods, allowing for new processes leading to higher future revenue for society. It is investment in the future. Say's prognosis was borne out in the Industrial Revolution, which saw a substantial increase in the amount of capital required to enable factories and railways to be built. Investment led to mass production and distribution in the 19th century. With the supply of necessities increasing dramatically, a substantial decrease in prices occurred, resulting in a deflationary boom. Today, we link deflation with depression, and we cannot envisage deflation in prices and a boom in production and employment occurring simultaneously. But this was not always so.[52]

John Maynard Keynes, in his chapter on investment in *The General Theory of Employment, Interest and Money*, highlights the importance of confidence in order to induce investment. He differentiates between the "serious-minded" investors looking at the long term and the "game players" or speculators, among whom he himself actually figured. In the 1930s following the crash, he writes that "investment based on genuine long-term expectation is so difficult today as to be scarcely practicable" and that "there is no clear evidence from experience that the investment policy which is socially advantageous coincides with that which is most profitable".[53] He notes that investors who focus on long-term fundamentals, while everyone else is engaged in short-term strategies, run greater risks.[54]

Keynes writes, however, that this speculative approach to investment would eventually fall away as wealth is built. From his 1930 essay we learn: "The love of money is detestable... We shall once more value ends above means and prefer the good to the useful."[55] He envisages a rather Utopian future of easy abundance with the benefit of money found in a joyful "art for living". We have still to wait for Keynes's prophecy to be fulfilled.[56] What does it entail for us? Is such a future indeed possible? Do we desire it? If so, how can we help construct it?

Restating the Human Purpose

Economic outcome is determined by human action and reaction. For this reason, Aristotle and other philosophers have been concerned with the way that human motivation influences economic outcome. Aristotle highlights the importance of the proportionality of exchange in markets, possible only through justice, the prevailing virtue. Locke stresses the importance of trust and stewardship in the development of property rights. For Smith, the self-regulating market is dependent not only on self-interest, but also self-command. Thus, we see the importance of virtue, or the ethics underlying economic activity.

For a well-functioning society, harmony is indispensable. Social harmony cannot be attained without wellbeing, possible only if the economy functions for the common good, with concern for the human being who is at the centre of economic activity. This entails reciprocity or friendship, and it implies that each economic agent has to do his part to contribute to the common purpose. This is not feasible without the practice of virtue which protects human dignity and contributes to prosperity for all. Individual action alone is insufficient; everyone must act in unison, each playing his part before a system of equal laws, of symmetry. Only thus can we arrive at not only equality and liberty, but fraternity and happiness, central human aspirations and key ideas contained in the American Declaration of Independence (1776), the rallying cry of the French Revolution (1789) and the Universal Declaration of Human Rights (1948). Only in this way can the invisible hand result and can we truly arrive at the ideal of economic prosperity espoused by Adam Smith.

Chapter 2

Constructive and Destructive Finance

"A constant in the history of money is that every remedy is reliably a source of new abuse."
John Kenneth Galbraith

"Speculative movements... are not irrelevant... they affect not only those who play the game but also those who never played at all."
George Akerlof and Robert Schiller

"For at least another hundred years we must pretend to ourselves and to everyone that fair is foul and foul is fair; for foul is useful and fair is not."
John Maynard Keynes

In the last chapter we examined the contribution of money and credit to the expansion of trade and markets and the flourishing of cities. We saw how debt allows for investment that creates future prosperity. Banks play a key role by intermediating and clearing financial transactions and providing funding for investment in business, projects, goods and services. In this chapter we will see how, with the era of 'financialization'[1] beginning in the 1980s, finance was transformed into an increasingly complex system and a powerful one, eventually unveiling a nefarious side. It evolved into the central engine for wealth creation, based on the belief that, by creating credit and hence money, banks would stimulate spending, benefiting the whole economy by expanding wealth. While this process initially contributed to a *virtuous* cycle, finance veered onto a path with certain destructive elements. Financial innovation permitted development of highly leveraged and opaque strategies. Short-term focus and deficient risk control, encouraged by excessive compensation practice, rendered the financial system fragile over time and caused damage to society, including increasing inequality.

Financialization and Deregulation

The process of financialization resulted from economic policy that started with a purpose. After the prosperous decades following World War II, the 1970s were problematic. The production engine was slowing. Investment and demand were faltering. Wealth creation faced resistance. Moreover, heretofore silent countries began to make a claim on wealth. The OPEC cartel of oil-producing countries was formed and the West could no longer set oil prices, which soared, leading to an inflationary spiral in commodity prices amidst depressed economic conditions. As a result, inflation reached double digits in the United States, Europe and many other countries. Stagflation was the order of the day. Under Paul Volcker, then Chairman of the US Federal Reserve Bank (the Fed), tight monetary policy[2] eventually contained inflation. The subsequent decline in interest rates, which had peaked in 1981, facilitated economic expansion.

Upon taking office, President Ronald Reagan and Prime Minister Margaret Thatcher saw the unleashing of market forces as the key to reviving economic activity, in the face of insufficient demand. Financial deregulation had begun in the United States with the liberalization of stock market commissions in 1975 and President Carter's Depository Institutions Deregulation and Monetary Control Act[3] in 1980, abolishing interest rate ceilings and permitting the expansion of mortgages and consumer credit. In the UK in 1986, deregulation of ownership of the London Stock Exchange resulted in the 'Big Bang'. Later the Glass-Steagall Act was repealed in 1999 in the USA – it had been introduced in 1933 to separate investment and commercial banking activities, following the financial folly of the 1920s, in order to safeguard against future excess.[4] In 2000, the Commodity Futures Modernization Act freed over-the-counter (OTC) derivatives between sophisticated parties from regulation as futures under the Commodity Exchange Act and as securities under the federal securities law.[5] These instruments would hereafter be supervised by federal regulators under general 'safe and soundness' principles.[6]

The Reagan era also saw the largest tax cut bill in American history, leading to major reductions in taxes on income and capital gains. In this way, market forces were fully unleashed to propel the economy forward. In the process, by 2005, the financial sector in the United States came to account for a record 40% of domestic profits, compared to 15% in the 1960s.[7] This percentage dropped after the financial crisis, and the economist Edward Yardeni reports the figure at about 22% in the third quarter of 2014.[8]

With an invigorated financial sector providing credit and favourable tax policy in the 1980s, investment was stimulated and production and jobs followed, increasing demand. Some called it trickle-down economics: wealth created at the top percolated down through the rest of society. A beneficial cycle continued for some time, with declining interest rates enabling greater debt service capacity, leading to robust borrowing, spending and investment. The invisible hand appeared to be working. However, over time, investment took on characteristics and objectives quite different from the beneficial ones intended at its conception.

Investment: Model and Markets

In *The Theory of Economic Development*, Joseph Schumpeter describes a beneficial investment model.[9] An entrepreneur innovates, and investment in his invention leads to job creation. The investor (bank and/or holder of financial wealth) provides credit or equity that makes such projects possible. Thus, capital is vital as it enables the entrepreneur to realize innovation.[10] Schumpeter points to the recurring cycle: innovation, imitation as success is recognized, institutionalization leading to a static state of equilibrium, and then a new round of innovation, which causes disruption of the old. He calls the whole process "creative destruction".

Schumpeter suggests that the motivation for innovation is complex and does not just involve profit, but also the creation and realization of a new and untested idea. The entrepreneur can be a "heroic" as well as an "economic" figure,[11] and plays a vital role as the creative agent: the innovator or inventor of the new business or process. The investor, by allowing innovation to be realized, contributes to economic stimulation, job creation and possibly improvement in living standards. Profit is indispensable as it confirms that the project merits the investment of money and permits it to continue. This approach to innovation and investment is beneficial to the economy and all parties gain: the entrepreneur, the investor, the worker, the supplier, the merchant and society in general.

At the beginning of the 1980s, credit expansion facilitated investment and spending and resulted in an economic boom. The entrepreneurial spirit, along with restructuring of corporations, led to economic expansion: higher profits, job creation and prosperity. Many industries were revived and businesses restructured and new ones created, all with a beneficial effect on employment. Technological innovation further contributed to efficiency gains, the creation of new businesses and economic stimulation. Investment in the property sector allowed for new construction and the restoration of buildings and regeneration of neighbourhoods and entire communities. The entry of emerging countries into the market contributed to economic growth and global prosperity. Wealth creation lifted many around the world out of poverty as markets and economies expanded. With cheap labour, Asia in particular benefited from entrepreneurship and direct investment which permitted the world to buy low-priced goods, keeping inflation at bay, while living standards rose globally.

In economic terms, this can be called a 'virtuous cycle', with credit expansion benefiting the real economy. This development led to increasing acceptance of the neo-classical model of free markets, motivated by self-interest and benefiting all – the invisible hand appeared to be at work. As a result, free markets were lauded and became entrenched and, with globalization, were seen to spread wealth worldwide.[12] Acknowledging the benefits of the policy cocktail of accommodative monetary policy and liberalization, countries across the world adopted this approach and the left/right divide in politics became fuzzy. The fall of Communism further fed infatuation with the neoliberal market system. The abandonment by Communists of anti-capitalist ideology reinforced the argument for unfettered markets and the invisible hand.

The financial system, through its creation of money, was seen as the engine behind this cycle of prosperity and, as a result, financial expansion and innovation were welcomed and encouraged worldwide, despite early indications of the risks arising from credit excess in the form of the Latin American debt crisis, which started in 1982. A further forewarning came with the Savings and Loans crisis in the United States in the mid-1980s, but it was ignored. The myth of beneficial self-regulating free markets was firmly entrenched and Milton Friedman and Friedrich Hayek, proponents of government non-intervention and market liberalization, became the economists of reference.[13] Outside their effect on economic growth, there was no need to consider the impact of markets on society or their long-term ramifications, for markets were self-regulating and efficient. They were 'perfect'. The invisible hand would ensure that everyone would gain.

Adair Turner, Chair of the United Kingdom's Financial Services Authority from 2008 until its abolition in 2013, noted that it had served everyone's interests to adopt blindly a single point of view: a "simple, constant and clearly communicated ideology" of market efficiency and investor rationality leading to equilibrium, with no room or need for regulation or discretionary stabilization. He termed this the "conventional wisdom" of perfect markets.[14] It had been adhered to by all: governments, regulators, banks, corporations, academics and investors. The market mantra which had taken hold had crept into all domains of life, including the daily life of the general public. It was accompanied by the belief that maximization of profit or money was the motivating and guiding factor and the life-generating force of the economy. This was in the participants' self-interest.

Expansion of Finance: Virtue to Vice

Within this ideological framework, financial markets played a central role. With inflation tamed, lower interest rates encouraged investment in bonds and in stocks. Tax reform gave this further impetus. The introduction of tax-beneficial retirement savings plans brought more investors into the market.[15] As profits rose and higher equity prices followed, stock market activity accelerated, with new participants and increased turnover. Furthermore, portfolio churning or trading to take advantage of price movements increased, including day-trading at the retail level. The equity bull market, which began in the United States in 1982, spread throughout the world.

Financial engineering, enhanced by technological advance, further fanned the flames of market activity. But not all financial innovation was beneficial and some had detrimental effects over time. An important early development was the emergence of leveraged buy-outs (LBOs) in the 1980s, made possible by the birth of the high-yield debt market, and undervalued corporate assets resulting from stagflation in the 1970s. Funded by debt (junk bonds paying high interest rates in a declining interest rate environment), private investors took over underpriced companies, often in a hostile fashion, and either stripped them, selling the components for more than the whole had cost, or brought the company back to market at a later date, issuing the shares at a premium.

LBO activity initially contributed to economic dynamism through the restructuring and optimization of inefficient businesses by giving them new life, as well as investment to enable growth. But at a later stage low interest rates continued to allow such activity, despite mature markets and even when companies were suitably priced and had no significant innovative potential. Under these circumstances, LBOs often contributed nothing to economic dynamism, even if they may have led to short-term improved efficiency due to lay-offs and asset-strips, resulting in profits for the new owners. In some cases, without a valid strategic plan to increase value for the firm, these buyouts over-burdened the companies with debt and led to their eventual demise.[16] Such companies were harmed by a conflict of interest between the financial objectives of the new owners and the long-term business objectives of the firm. As a result, businesses faltered and employees were hurt by job losses or a deterioration in employment conditions, with a consequent impact on local communities.

Another important development was the expansion of derivatives. This allowed for bigger and more intensive bets on investment markets and the proliferation of hedge funds. Referring to derivatives, Alan Greenspan, Chairman of the Fed from 1987 to 2006 and advocate of 'perfect' markets, said: "These instruments enhance the ability to differentiate risk and allocate it to those investors most able and willing to take it".[17] Derivatives did indeed contribute to more effective exposure management and enabled financial professionals to protect their commodity, currency, interest rate and general investment exposure.

However, while the protection they offered against investment exposure was beneficial, derivatives expanded effective leverage to highly risky and unsustainable levels, and permitted speculation on assets not owned by the speculator.[18] Although derivatives may have increased liquidity, they added to market risk and made possible an explosion in 'virtual investment', removed from industrial and commercial transactions, but moving in tandem with the underlying instruments. Such positions added no value to the real economy,[19] but instead magnified market risk exponentially. The increasing complexity, opacity and exponential growth of derivatives played a large part in the financial meltdown of 2008.[20]

The high-tech revolution of the 1990s facilitated financial trading and innovation for the enhancement of investment returns. While some strategies were sensible and useful, technological innovation allowed for the development of complex strategies, based on algorithms and using derivatives that were not founded on sound principles and difficult to comprehend, thereby opening up opportunities for predatory exploitation. The speed at which money could be created (and spun) increased. Restraint, responsibility and trust dissipated. Greed was magnified, extraction of income by certain groups increased, and in some cases fraud followed.

Abuse revealed in the financial sector includes LIBOR fixing, collusion in foreign exchange and gold markets, insider trading, rigging of stock markets, and mis-selling of mortgage securities and other financial instruments, including investment and banking products and insurance to the retail sector. Since it is easy to be enamoured of wealth not earned through dedicated work but increasingly conjured up as if by magic, lessons from past speculative bubbles were ignored and values forgotten. Money-creation had become too easy for some; the temptation was great.

As the risk profile of financial activity advanced and grew to dangerous levels, a series of bubbles resulted: the Asian debt crisis in 1997, the Long-Term Capital Management[21] fiasco in 1998, the dot-com bubble of 2000-2001, and eventually the subprime mortgage scandal leading to the major financial crisis of 2008. By continuously providing liquidity to prevent major financial disruption, the Fed propped up what would reveal itself to be a fragile financial system. While preventing immediate economic pain, Fed action had the perverse effect of protecting and, thus, encouraging excessive risk-taking and allowing asset bubbles to inflate again and again. Moral hazard was entrenched.

When the dot-com crisis erupted in 2000, declining interest rates and aggressive bank lending led to the real estate bubble that followed. Speculators gained in confidence and risk-taking accelerated, encouraging new players to enter the game and participate in easy profits, leading to a pattern of ease, boom and bust that continued until the major crisis in 2008. The risk remains of similar patterns building up again, as warned by the Bank for International Settlements in its Annual Report in June 2014.[22]

Securitization of mortgages, beginning on a wide scale in the 1990s, was another important financial development that had started beneficially, by facilitating access to credit, particularly for first-time home-buyers. However, the acceleration of the process between 2004 and 2007, assisted by the development of derivatives, permitted the introduction of subprime mortgages of dismal quality, frequently offered to people without the capacity to understand them or the credit standing to assume them,[23] and encouraged detrimental real estate speculation. Securitization of mortgages allowed banks to pay scant attention to credit quality since the mortgages were sold off in tranches to other investors and removed from the bank's balance sheet.[24]

Investor laxity in credit assessment was fuelled by the assumption that rating agencies would serve as guardians of credit quality. But they failed to assess credit risk adequately and even attributed AAA ratings to unsound instruments that could have been rated 'junk'.[25] A conflict of interest was at play: credit agencies depended on banks for revenues and were keen to keep the activity churning by safeguarding their clients' placement ability with high instrument ratings. The true risk profile was further masked by insurance companies willing to provide guarantees against credit default.

Rather than providing risk protection, credit default swaps (CDSs)[26] can, in fact, increase risk. CDSs allow for a main requirement in the investment decision to be ignored, that of risk analysis and control, and provide an avenue for speculation. Junk can be bought and protected by an overlay of CDSs; and CDSs can be purchased without any underlying credit investment position, as a 'play' to capitalize on expected movements in credit pricing, arising from a change in risk perception or interest rate direction. In other words, punters could purchase CDSs, even if they had no underlying investment to protect. In this way, their bet on a change in credit standing or interest rate direction could realize them profits if proven to be correct. These speculative investment plays, known as 'naked CDSs', arose from derivatives and reinforced their explosive increase.[27]

Thus, in the lead-up to the subprime fiasco, risk control was often ignored, underestimated or misunderstood at all levels: by real estate developers and agents in promoting speculation, by commercial banks in not practising due diligence in loan assessments, by borrowers themselves in taking on debt beyond their capacity to service it, by investment banks in issuing collateralized debt securities that carried exceptionally high risk without transparency, by credit-rating agencies in attributing high ratings to paper of questionable quality, by insurance companies in underwriting debt cover on such securities beyond the level of risk tolerance, and by investors in accepting high-risk paper in their portfolio as a consequence of blind trust and complacency in risk assessment and often a desire to maximize short-term gains.

Particularly worrisome was the subsequent exposure that unethical and fraudulent behaviour contributed to the financial meltdown. Investment banks were found to have sold mortgage-backed securities in full knowledge of their toxic characteristics and plans by agents to short them aggressively, contributing to an inevitable crash in their price levels.[28] And retail banks were discovered to have mis-sold pension, insurance and other products to their clients.[29] Both sophisticated and unsophisticated investors paid a high price for their participation, and even those not directly involved suffered financial losses when the meltdown occurred through economic impact. No one was spared.

We can see that while expanded financial participation did initially contribute to beneficial economic growth, untrammelled financial expansion and misplaced technological innovation eventually damaged the virtuous cycle, by removing finance from underlying economic reality and needs, moving it further and further into the virtual realm. The investment time frame shortened and sophisticated strategies were sought to keep returns at unjustifiable and unsustainable levels. All this activity happened in the face of supervisory complacency. It was true that deregulation had facilitated such practices, but it was equally true that the regulations still in place were not properly enforced, and that the monitoring of safe and sound principles fell away. In the euphoria, many turned a blind eye so that the boom could continue. No one wanted to be outside the money-spinning game and no one dared to think differently or to detonate a fragile engine. Chuck Prince, then CEO of Citicorp famously told the *Financial Times* in July 2007: "When the music stops, in terms of liquidity, things will be complicated. But as long as the music is playing, you've got to get up and dance. We're still dancing."[30]

In the financial frenzy, the benefit of debt in facilitating investment for improving future economic prospects was forgotten, and its use for such purposes was bypassed with growing frequency. Debt became a means to finance consumption or to increase paper wealth; repayment dates were continuously pushed forward into the future. Increasing levels of debt had to be conjured up in order to feed the economic engine and maintain ever-increasing consumption and improved living standards. Growth was founded not on a solid investment base, but on an ever-growing debt bubble, which brought incredible riches to some who knew how to exploit it, but a weakened financial edifice for all.

Turning Finance Toxic

Finance as the engine of wealth creation had the nefarious effect of shifting the focus of investment from beneficial economic expansion and entrepreneurial innovation for job creation to innovation for paper wealth creation. Speculation played a major role. Mimicry of destructive behaviour, not of the beneficial type described in Schumpeter's thesis of creative destruction, expanded the vicious cycle in the financial world. Milton Friedman had written in defence of speculation, arguing that it does not destabilize markets, because "people who destabilize the market lose their shirts, so they aren't going to be around for long".[31] However, on the contrary, people who destabilized the market in recent times have walked away with fortunes maintained,[32] while leaving the responsible, innocent and powerless suffering the consequences of the mess. Like Friedrich Hayek,[33] Friedman believes that speculation plays an indispensable role in 'price discovery', in the midst of dispersed information. This argument continues today as a justification for speculation, but it requires further examination.

Hayek writes that an economic problem facing society is the full utilization of knowledge, not given to anyone in its totality and often held in contradictory forms. He argues that speculation helps determine prices more efficiently by relying on market forces rather than central planning. He expounds: "The shipper who earns his living from using otherwise empty or half-filled journeys of tramp-steamers, or the estate agent whose whole knowledge is almost exclusively one of temporary opportunities, or the arbitrageur who gains from local differences of commodity prices, are all performing eminently useful functions based on special knowledge of circumstances of the fleeting moment not known to others... The whole acts as one market, not because any of its members survey the whole field, but because their limited individual fields of vision sufficiently overlap so that through many intermediaries the relevant information is communicated to all."

This rationale applies to legitimate speculation, which enables price determination in trade and commerce, supported by underlying economic activity. This set of conditions is quite different from that of paper speculation unsupported by underlying physical assets, often involving asymmetrical information and market manipulation,[34] in order to capitalize on directional shifts and thereby adding volatility to financial markets and instability to the system, all compounded by leverage. Hayek would probably not have approved of such speculation. Thus, it is not necessarily speculation *per se* that is detrimental, but the purpose behind the speculation. Is it justifiable or not? Does it provide real economic value? Does it help to perfect markets or to destroy them? Can it in fact be harmful?

Robert Shiller defines a speculative bubble as "a situation in which news of price increases spurs investor enthusiasm, which spreads by psychological contagion from person to person, in the process amplifying stories that might justify the price increases and bringing in a larger and larger class of investors who, despite doubts about the real value of an investment, are drawn to it partly through envy of others' successes and partly through a gambler's excitement".[35] He uses 'feed-back loop theory' to show how initial price increases caused by precipitating factors lead to further price increases as the effects of initial price movements feed back into yet higher prices by fanning investor demand. Each round of price increases causes yet another round through increased but unjustified investor confidence.[36] He refers to this as a vicious cycle in popular terms. Feed-back loop dynamics generate complex and even apparently random behaviour. Thus, we see that markets are neither rational, efficient nor perfect. On the contrary, they can be irrational, inefficient and viciously destructive.

Hyman Minsky brings us back to basics with his 'financial instability hypothesis',[37] which had been mostly forgotten until the 2008 crisis reminded us all of it. He argues that debt and capital asset acquisitions can only be justified by future cash flow in the form of profits or increased income. Otherwise a financial crisis results when assets have to be sold to realize cash. Minsky describes Ponzi finance as a situation where income falls short of interest payments and cash flow falls short of capital commitments. So, a Ponzi scheme has to increase its outstanding debt in order to meet its obligations. Sometimes fraud is involved.[38]

Minsky elaborates that during a period of prosperity and full employment, a decline in liquidity preference (investors feel less need to have cash available) causes a shift in portfolio preference to capital assets (people prefer to invest cash in stocks, bonds, property, etc.), thus giving rise to an increase in prices. This price increase invites greater speculation and can lead to Ponzi-like conditions that are both adopted by investors and accepted by bankers. In other words, stability can breed instability. At some juncture, the initial short-term cash flow deficit is recognized as permanent, and the bubble bursts. He further contends that inflation is one way to ease debt payment commitments and warns that if government stands ready to provide guarantees against investment losses, levels of foolish investment increase.[39] This leads to 'moral hazard' and eventually to a collapse in asset prices, known popularly as the 'Minsky moment'. He proposes the simplification of financial structures as a way to achieve greater stability.

Our financial structures are not simple. The financial reality is revealed to be even more lethal than we might imagine through the kind of corruption exposed by Michael Lewis in his book, *Flash Boys: Cracking the Money Code.* High frequency traders are justified as market makers, but Lewis shows how technology has enabled the unscrupulous to manipulate information flows, thus trading profitably in anticipation of stock orders. Lewis explains that because of trades sent to different exchanges where executions are made sequentially, and because of minute differences in travel time, those with early access to information about orders can exploit it for advantageous trading. In his study, Lewis determined that differences in travel time were minute, as was the total travel time,[40] and yet greater speed allowed for profitable trading. Lewis writes of traders willing to pay brokers to see order flows and banks spending vast sums of money to find the most efficient routes for their orders and the best machines to anticipate stock market trades. Immense sums of money and valuable time have been committed in order to achieve financial advantage, without serving any useful purpose.

Frenetic trading, seen as a sign of technological progress, has revealed itself to entail market rigging and pecuniary losses to legitimate investors. As Lewis explains, "speed led to money", and he estimates that this market exploitation could cost the investment community tens of billions of dollars per annum.[41] And we see that requisite regulatory supervision renders the cost even higher to all,[42] without necessarily resolving the problem. Lewis writes that the stock market, which began as a mechanism for channelling capital to productive enterprise, has become a black box with inner workings that elude understanding. Complexity is designed to allow predatory action.

A sinister practice that Lewis unveiled in his book exists within 'dark pools' at banks where clients' orders are matched outside the market, as a first stopping point for trades.[43] Inside these dark pools, opportunities exist for trading to exploit clients' orders or selling to high-frequency traders early access to order information.[44] Lawsuits have been filed and fines imposed by the Attorney General of New York State against such practices.[45] Legitimate position-taking through arbitrage, to exploit price differentials arising from disparate knowledge, involves risk-taking. With arbitrage, the outcome is unknown. 'Front-running' is risk-free and guarantees profit. It is also illegal.

Misguided Finance and Income Disparity

Contributing to the explosive build-up in the financial sector was the advent of excessive banking bonuses, with an incentive system based on a percentage of revenues or profits.[46] While a bonus system that permits alignment of interest with no detriment to society is justified, what emerged instead was the introduction of abusive excess into the system. Attracted by high compensation, brilliant mathematicians and physicists moved to Wall Street and the City, and other productive sectors of the economy were deprived of their contribution. Despite their brilliance with mathematics, algorithms and computer modelling, the risk profile of many of their investment strategies was not adequately analysed or was conveniently ignored, and the system was at times manipulated for advantage. The compensation allure was indeed great and the pressure to increase revenues high. This *modus operandi* disconnected many in finance from the real world.[47] Sebastian Faulks[48] recounts an interesting tale of a delusional world which has inflicted damage on our financial edifice. An illustrative excerpt appears at the end of this chapter.

We can trace the origin of the outsized bonus culture to the 1980s. Leveraged buyouts (LBOs) contributed to an escalation in executive compensation through participation in enhanced share value. The corporate world believed handsome compensation motivated executives to maximize share prices – a desired objective. Moreover, higher share prices helped discourage takeovers by making them more costly, and linking compensation to stock prices gave executives an effective stake in the company, deterring them also from conspiring to take over their own firm. Over time a compensation structure became installed in the corporate world to reward executives even when no real value was provided. The justification was that the firm had to 'remain competitive', and executive consultants reinforced this myth, as it also benefitted them to do so – a prime example of conflict of interest, where their own interests and those of senior executives were met, but not necessarily those of the client firm as a whole. As a result, senior corporate managers saw their compensation packages increase exponentially. In the United States, in 1970 the pay of a chief executive was under 30 times that of the average worker; by 2010 it was 263 times.[49]

In the banking sector, mergers and acquisitions (M&A) began to provide huge fees through deal making. To encourage an expansion of banking activity, leading to fees and profits, the bonus system was extended across banks. As a result, product development and trading grew, eventually overshadowing M&A, and led to the creation of explosively toxic investment products, increasing leverage, weakening risk control and even the abandonment of fiduciary responsibility. The bonus culture shifted the focus for assessing executive performance from long-term strategic design for economic benefit and long-term growth to share price maximization and short-term gain.

Myopic investment strategies led to a decline in the average holding period of securities for institutional portfolios from seven years in the 1960s to under a year by the end of the 20th century.[50] Instead of financing real growth, investment often turned to money churning, permitted by financial engineering and virtual markets. Trading, helped by speculation, became the investment strategy of choice for many and contributed to bank returns through brokerage commissions and profitable trading for the bank's proprietary account.

The financial and investment approach that resulted has contributed to volatility and prejudiced long-term performance. Extreme swings in share prices, while favouring trading, make it difficult for investors to increase their investment assets in a gradual fashion, in line with business activity and economic development for long-term benefit. Determining intrinsic equity value becomes increasingly difficult. Robert Shiller notes: "Unknown to most investors is the troubling lack of credibility in the quality of research being done on the stock market, to say nothing of the clarity and accuracy with which it is communicated to the public. Some of this so-called research often seems no more rigorous than the reading of tea leaves."[51] And he questions whether investors simply fulfil their own prophecy by mimicking each other. With lack of clarity and magnified risk, making decisions about saving and investment becomes an anxiety-provoking exercise for the typical person, who needs to provide for retirement.

Financial practice has contributed to income disparity and inequality, seen today as one of our greatest challenges.[52] Thomas Piketty in his watershed book, *Capital in the 21st Century,* points to a "fundamental force of divergence" as a principal cause of rising inequality. He writes that when the return on capital is higher than economic growth ($r > g$), the divergence in income is likely to set in motion accelerated capital accumulation.[53] As the wealthy are able to add to their investment base, since returns exceed consumption needs, the wealth disparity is further magnified. Piketty concludes that other than during the thirty golden or glorious years (*les trentes glorieuses*) from 1945 to 1975, rising inequality has been the norm, going as far back as 1800.[54] The exceptional period of income compression was due to the destruction of wealth by war and progressive taxation, as well as high income growth across society due to post-war reconstruction, population growth and welfare policy. Workers gained bargaining position, supported by government action. Piketty argues that political and economic changes are inextricably intertwined and hence favours the term 'political economy'.

However, Piketty does not point to the full effect of the transformation of the financial paradigm on recent wealth divergence. While he criticizes high executive compensation and calls this a reason for rising wealth disparity, the cause goes beyond bonuses. The financial boom starting in the 1980s led to very high returns on financial assets and real estate, and leverage amplified these returns. While exceptional returns may have been justified in the early 1980s, when the starting investment base was undervalued and productive restructuring provided real value creation, persistent high returns today may no longer be justifiable or sustainable, other than in specific cases where long-term profits are created and real value to the economy added. Yet the pursuit of exceptionally high returns persists. In the case of LBOs, we have seen, as just described, that this is now often possible with an approach that runs directly counter to the interests of the firm and employees. In other cases, exceptional returns often arise through speculation or even market manipulation. Excessive financial rent-seeking can cause fragility and be a serious detriment to the economic and financial system.

Our investment model favours the creation of financial paper wealth rather than fixed investment and job creation. And a large part of real estate investment simply involves a flipping or change in ownership and not new construction. We have seen extended bull market periods in financial instruments and property, with several crashes in the interim and a particularly large one in 2008, followed by rebounds in all cases. The sophisticated investor is savvy in navigating these waters but the average investor is less astute and does not have access to the same level of expertise or information, or even access to credit for financing such investments. More powerful investors have achieved preferential returns from the market.[55] As such, with limited job creation and a lower participation by the majority in income growth, the financialization process has accentuated income inequality,[56] but it has also caused money to be less productive.[57] Investment is not leading to improved economic prospects across the board.

Tragedy of the Financial Commons

We can view our financial edifice as our financial commons, which should provide benefit to all. Garrett Hardin's 'Tragedy of the Commons'[58] can be adapted to illustrate the financial damage of recent times. In Hardin's essay, he describes how an area of common land can be depleted if all members of the community use it for grazing their own cattle, without concern for its preservation. He uses this analogy to illustrate environmental degradation and it has become a metaphor of reference. In a similar fashion, the executive compensation system and excessive return requirements, which encourage high leverage, a short-term focus, destructive speculation, and even predatory manipulation, rather than beneficial long-term investment, have allowed certain asset owners and agents in the business and financial sectors to benefit while rendering the economic and financial system fragile. In short, through money making and rent extraction, wealth has not only been appropriated from the common pool by a minority, but this action has left a damaged and diminished commons for the majority: a bleak reality and poor prognosis for the future. This is manifested through increasing inequality and the fragile financial system we inhabit.

Finance is not serving society today. In the course of the past thirty years, financial innovation designed with the explicit purpose of meeting perceived requirements and expanding participation has decoupled finance from underlying economic activity and led to a series of bets that have been destructive to society.[59] True to James Tobin's prophecy in 1984, casino finance took hold. Tobin had warned: "Deregulation should not be viewed as a routine application of free market philosophy... Rather it should be guided by sober pragmatic consideration of what we can reasonably expect the financial system to achieve and at what social cost." He confessed to an uneasy suspicion that "we are throwing more and more of our resources, including... our youth, into activities that generate high private rewards disproportionate to their social productivity. I suspect that the immense power of the computer is being harnessed to this paper economy, not to do the same transactions more economically but to balloon the quantity and variety of financial exchanges... I fear that, as Keynes saw... the advantages of the liquidity and negotiability of financial instruments come at the cost of facilitating n^{th}-degree speculation which is short sighted and inefficient."[60] Thirty years ago we did not heed Tobin's prophecy, and now the issue has become critical. Financial expansion focuses on instrumental efficiency, justified by liquidity, and neglects social cost.

With the shift of financial emphasis from beneficial investment towards money making, while Adam Smith's self-interest has been maintained, his self-command, or sense of responsibility to the financial commons, has been forgotten. As a result, the invisible hand has stopped working. In his 2003 book, *The Roaring Nineties: Seeds of Destruction*,[61] Joseph Stiglitz, like Tobin, warns that the shift in focus – from real economic benefit to society towards money making – has contributed to a misplaced motivation and award system, which would lead to societal disintegration: "America bought the general line of the market economy: compensation reflected productivity. Those who were paid more were contributing more to society. It was natural that young people would be attracted to the frenzy. They could do well for society by doing well for themselves."[62] He denounces the liberal market ideology and focus on money-making and calls for a proper balance between the individual and society to be brought back. The question of what true self-interest implies and the importance of self-command in order to bring about the operation of the invisible hand is of concern in this book.

Misplaced self-interest and irrational behaviour led to the creation of disparate wealth and multiple bubbles, weakening the security net for many and causing a crisis of confidence and a financial *modus operandi* that renders the financial edifice fragile and the social situation potentially explosive. It also makes investing for the future difficult. A beneficial investment model does not entail short-term speculation and trading for money-making, but encourages sound asset allocation and diversification into productive and solid assets, enabling participation in beneficial economic growth and wealth creation for all. To achieve this, the behaviour of financial agents and investors will have to change, transferring the focus to solid long-term investment and restoring trust and confidence through responsible action. A reformed motivational structure in finance will facilitate the process, but we cannot underestimate cultural change. Otherwise, an investment model with lasting benefits will remain elusive, inequality will continue to rise and the financial commons will remain damaged.

Requisite Reform

Imperfect markets and the resulting crisis led to an increasing call for legislation, which resulted in the Dodd-Frank Act, passed by the US Congress in 2010. In an article in 2012, *The Economist* illustrates the absurdity of complex legislation,[63] whereby banks and their lawyers seek exploitation of loopholes, while governments expend energy and money on closing them.[64] Such a bureaucratic nightmare paralyses effective supervision and requisite action. In fact, it wastes intellectual and financial resources. It is *inefficient.* Although the Volcker rule has since been passed,[65] resistance to meaningful reform remains, and it is not clear that recent financial scandals have reduced the banks' lobbying position.[66] However, the determination exhibited by the SEC and other regulatory authorities to hold banks accountable and their success in effecting prosecution, particularly in the USA and the UK, together with public pressure, may yet lead eventually to reform. Policy, regulation and supervision make up the macro-prudential pillar of the financial system.

The second pillar, the micro-prudential, involves management, risk control and bank solvency. Basel III, which governs financial structure and calls for increased levels of bank capital in relation to total assets, makes an important contribution, even if it is hard to fathom.[67] Pointing to the risks that banks assume which may not be adequately reflected in their balance sheets, Anat Admati and Martin Hellwig argue for higher capital levels in their book, *The Bankers' New Clothes: What's Wrong with Banking and What to Do About It.* Using the example of JP Morgan Chase, they show that the "fortress balance sheet" referred to by its CEO, Jamie Dimon, is not that resilient when certain off-balance sheet items, primarily derivatives, are fully accounted for and not netted off.[68] They posit that the appropriate debt/equity mix seen as prudent for corporations should also apply to banks, suggesting that equity be in the order of 20-30% of total assets.[69] Admati and Hellwig say that reform has been stalled by the banking industry promoting the view that the sector is a special case and not subject to the necessary constraints applied to other businesses and by a lack of resolve to challenge the sector, for fear that banking restraint would harm lending and growth. We have seen throughout our discussion the central role that finance plays in the economy, though it is not always a beneficial one.

Whatever supervision and management are implemented at both the macro- and micro-levels, the financial system will remain faulty without the third pillar, appropriate behaviour. Responsible agents are indispensable. Mark Carney, Governor of the Bank of England, and Christine Lagarde, Managing Director of the International Monetary Fund, both highlighted this point in a conference on Inclusive Capitalism in London in May, 2014.[70] In her speech, Lagarde refers to excess in risk-taking, leverage, complexity, opacity and compensation, all leading to massive destruction in value and contributing to high unemployment, social tensions and political disillusionment.[71] Not only for bankers and regulators, but for all players, including investors[72] and borrowers,[73] i.e. for the public at large, action determines financial outcome. Until trust is restored through responsible action at all levels, no amount of legislation can correct the situation and make finance beneficial. In their book, *Animal Spirits: How Human Psychology Drives the Economy and Why It Matters for Global Capitalism*, George Akerlof and Robert Shiller write that the financial economy "cannot be described solely by considering economic motives... [but] also requires detailed understanding of confidence, of fairness, of opportunities for corruption, of money illusion and of stories that are handed to us by history".[74]

Akerlof and Shiller link economic depressions to overheated economies arising from a growth in corrupt practice and the subsequent collapse in confidence. They include the US depression of the 1890s and the global depression of the 1930s, "characterized by fundamental changes in confidence in the economy, in the willingness to press pursuit of profit to antisocial limits, in money illusion, and in changes in the perception of economic fairness".[75] Recent economic and financial setbacks can be traced to corruption scandals: the savings and loan crisis of the 1980s and 1990s, the

Enron scandal in 2001, and the subprime mortgage crisis beginning in 2007. In all the situations Akerlof and Shiller analysed, fear arising from bad faith and corruption led to a breakdown of trust and a collapse of confidence, as well as a sense of unfairness. Today, the breakdown of trust[76] and the spread of corruption worldwide[77] pose a big challenge.

The Future of Finance: What Shape or Design?

We are at a crossroads in relation to economic and financial theory. Alan Greenspan himself acknowledged that classic orthodox economics and mathematical models can no longer explain everything, for in September 2008 the venerated models suddenly stopped working.[78] Greenspan questioned whether there are alternative ways to forecast the economy, if classic models were no longer infallible. He delved into behavioural economics, anthropology and psychology, including the work of Daniel Kahneman, but felt those fields "did not offer a magic wand". While economic models still work in terms of predicting behaviour in the *real* economy – in tangible items like inventories – he says that money is another matter. To quote Greenspan: "Finance is wholly different from the rest of the economy". More specifically, while markets sometimes behave in ways that models might predict, they can also become 'irrational', defying mathematics. We can deduce that behaviour is as important as theory and financial models in determining financial outcome.

Keynes, whose ideas held sway in the first half of the 20th century, and who is regaining visibility, believed in government action to counter the volatile effect of human behaviour, characterized by 'animal spirits'. Beginning in the 1970s, neo-classical economists led by Friedman and Hayek removed erratic human behaviour from economic consideration. They believed that in an "extended order" (the dispersed and globalized capitalistic system) abstract theory had to provide the answer, and that free and liberal markets were best placed to further wealth for all. To counter economic stagnation, finance was deemed a pivotal tool for wealth creation. As markets were assumed to be rational and self-correcting, i.e.

perfect, they could be free and unfettered. This led to successive financial bubbles building up and to the largest 'burst' ever in 2008, leaving disruption across all markets and many banks verging on bankruptcy, until government stepped in to the rescue. Wealth creation was assumed to benefit all,[79] but this theory has proved faulty and inequality has risen.

Since the crisis, government action has contributed to a restoration of bank capital in the United States through an extensive injection of capital and liquidity into the system,[80] helping to bring shaky banks back to health. In Europe, however, financial health has yet to return. The challenge here is more difficult, due to the sharing of a single non-reserve currency by various governments with different financial policies and objectives. Austerity has been the focus, in the midst of public resistance. This is starting to change with the promise of quantitative easing in Europe. The complexity of the European situation does not allow us to treat it in any detail in this book. However, the challenges that Europe faces in reforming finance are the same as those in the USA, the UK and across the world.

The global financial debate today is centred on deciding an appropriate debt policy. Economists arguing for debt restraint include Carmen Reinhart and Kenneth Rogoff, who point to systemic risks arising from excessive debt in their book, *This Time is Different: Eight Centuries of Financial Folly*. They draw parallels between the past and our recent debt explosion, arguing that this time is *not* different, contrary to the sanguine approach taken before the crisis, as a result of confidence in financial innovation and globalization and the beneficial characteristics of the USA's large and liquid financial markets.[81] In a later paper, they write that when government debt reaches a certain level (established at 90%),[82] untenable interest expense burdens serve as a long-term brake on economic growth. Critics have since moved to discredit their analysis following exposure by students of statistical error in their work,[83] thus adding weight to a pro-debt argument that causation is backwards, that lower growth actually leads to higher debt-to-GDP ratios.

Gillian Tett believes that the financial problem cannot be fixed without tackling 'debt addiction'.[84] She refers to a speech by Adair Turner[85] in which he says that the traditional role of banks (which is to take deposits, in order to fund investment) is no longer applicable. In the UK, only 15% of financial flows go into investment projects. The rest support existing corporate assets, real estate or unsecured personal finance to "facilitate lifestyle consumption smoothing". Turner notes that some non-investment finance is socially useful, but the bulk is not, and points to the declining productivity of money as debt escalates while growth remains flat. He questions the sustainability of a system that requires ever-growing debt.[86] Until this is resolved, policy makers will simply be propping up an unstable system. Turner calls for a radical overhaul of economic and financial models.

In defence of civil rights and social benefits gained, including education, social mobility and home ownership, Mark Blyth argues that liquidity to enable growth is indispensable, and uses his own beneficial example to argue his case. He maintains that the USA is immune to any sovereign debt crisis, since it controls its own currency. Attributing the financial crisis of 2008 not to debt *per se* but to banking behaviour and moral hazard, he contrasts liquidity with austerity as a potential solution.[87] He is justified in arguing that over-borrowing is possible only with over-lending. However, we have seen how massive liquidity injections by central banks can feed moral hazard and fan speculation in housing and financial markets.[88]

The Bank for International Settlements (BIS), in its 2014 Annual Report, points to the danger of excessive Central Bank easing, which has propelled asset prices again to dangerously high levels, while having insufficient impact on job creation.[89] The BIS points to risks of secular stagnation, as both private and public debt continue to rise. It urges a move away from debt as the engine of growth, towards addressing structural deficiencies and resource misallocations. However, Andy Haldane, the Chief Economist of the Bank of England, defends central bank policy in a "nutty world", as the "alternative would be nuttier still".[90] Has financialization so entrenched debt creation that moderation cannot be introduced back into the system?

Defending Fed policy in a 2014 speech, Janet Yellen speaks of the significant limitations of monetary policy in promoting financial stability, as its effects on financial vulnerabilities, such as excessive leverage and maturity transformation, are not well understood. She argues that it should be the job of macroprudential supervision and regulation to guard stability.[91] Yet we cannot overlook the risks arising from the unintended consequences of easy money. If the market is flooded with liquidity, how should it be used? Should we be sanguine about credit creation? Can the fragility of our financial system be resolved by pumping liquidity?[92] Can we afford not to give appropriate attention, not only to financial architecture, but also to human behaviour?

Martin Wolf, in his book, *The Shifts and the Shocks,* refers to an inherent contradiction between macroprudential regulation and monetary policy. While the former seeks to restrain over-leverage, the latter might, in the aftermath of an economic downturn arising from financial crisis, call for the lowering of interest rates and borrowing, so as to get the economy going again.[93] In fact, this is what we saw after the high-tech bubble collapse, leading to the subprime excess, and again after the financial fiasco of 2008. While acknowledging the importance of getting the recovery on track in the short term, in order to avoid a long-term loss of output, Wolf emphasizes the need for radical reform in the long run, so as to make the financial system resilient and to minimize any detrimental impact on the economy.

Wolf shares the opinion that dependence on debt creation as the engine of growth has led to financial fragility. He believes that the path traced by government implies maintenance of the pre-crisis financial model, albeit with greater financial regulation and macroprudential supervision. As such, this 'new orthodoxy' will not lead to long-term financial sustainability. He suggests going further in order to address major fault lines, some of which we have already discussed, such as further reinforcement of capital.[94] He recommends incorporating an equity feature into debt, including participation by the mortgage holder in any change in property value, as this would make for more sustainable debt creation. Further measures to encourage equity rather than debt include tax reform, such as elimination of the tax-deductibility of interest or some alternative to render debt and equity more tax-neutral. Reform of corporate taxation may help resolve the 'global savings glut' and 'investment dearth', by encouraging investment, thus reducing the excessive liquidity found on corporate balance sheets. Deficient corporate governance, including the executive bonus system that rewards short-term stock price performance, such as through share buybacks, will have to be addressed.

Along with many public figures, Wolf acknowledges income inequality as a major challenge for our times.[95] This can be addressed through tax reform, but more interestingly he suggests it be done through direct payment to the public via creation of money by government, in line with the Chicago Plan proposed in the 1930s and entailing 100% reserve banking.[96] The monetary system is both a social contrivance and a public good. Such direct money creation will help address structurally deficient demand and provide support to the economy, without adding fragility to the system through higher debt levels. Beyond a certain point, growth in debt no longer adds value or real wealth.

Here we need to raise again the issue of the nature and quality of growth. It has to be intelligent. We will see in the next chapter the inherent contradictions in economic growth, as we understand it, in serving society. Wolf raises many other interesting and disturbing issues about the nature of finance and its future that are outside the scope of this book. However, we should note his critical view of the destabilizing effect of "huge sums of liquid finance... [moving] around the world, most of it managed by agents rewarded for achieving short-term gains"[97] and the loss of trust in financial and political governance.[98] This view is in line with our discussion of the role of money and the economy and the requirements of the social contract. Finance has become destructive in recent times;

we need to make it constructive again. In order to do so, we must understand how finance is to serve not only the financial world, but society at large.

The current debate around appropriate monetary and debt policy is indeed too vast and complex to be covered adequately here. It involves famous economists and important institutions taking different and sometimes opposing views.[99] Even Greenspan has admitted to being at a loss as to what the future course of finance should be[100] and Yellen to a lack of experience and inadequacy in understanding the effect of monetary policy on financial stability. We are exploring uncharted territory in an inexact science. Martin Wolf's book helps us understand the complexity of the links between economics and finance and to see how any remedy entails many facets that need to be adequately understood and controlled. It is an impossible task to provide any sure proof or perfect solution. Therefore, it must perforce be accompanied by human responsibility. If the motivation of self-interest, as used in liberal economics, has been proven faulty, what is to take its place?

Our financial and economic paradigm in recent times has increasingly counted on the wealth effect to promote growth. Such wealth has come from money creation and rising asset prices, rather than sustained economic improvement. It may help feed consumption and thus contribute to economic growth, but it also leads to inequality and financial instability and even environmental degradation. If the wealth effect is not founded on anything solid, ever-increasing debt could cause a repeat of the painful bubble of 2008 and perhaps a more devastating one. In *Finance and the Good Society,* Robert Shiller writes that financial theory focuses on the short term, on portfolio optimization via trading strategies and risk management; however, financial professionals can be involved in constructive deal-making, in the structuring of projects, enterprises and systems. He describes finance as "the science of goal architecture – of the structuring of the economic arrangements necessary to achieve a set of goals and of the stewardship of the assets needed for that achievement".[101]

Yes, finance should concern itself with stewardship. Alan Blinder draws up Ten Financial Commandments shown on the next page.[102] Just as Shiller refers to financial stewardship, the commandments involve sound financial principles. However, even if Blinder does not put faith in self-regulation (Commandment No. 2), we should not underestimate human potential. In fact, I would suggest that self-regulation, called self-command by Adam Smith, is indispensable.

Alan Blinder's Ten Financial Commandments

1. Thou shalt remember that people forget
2. Thou shalt not rely on self-regulation
3. Thou shalt honour thy shareholders
4. Thou shalt elevate the importance of risk management
5. Thou shalt use less leverage
6. Thou shalt keep it simple, stupid (modern finance thrives on complexity) – rely on good judgment, transparency and market discipline if there is any
7. Thou shalt standardize derivatives and trade them on organized exchanges
8. Thou shalt keep things on the Balance Sheet
9. Thou shalt fix perverse compensation systems (this should be enforced by CEOs and corporate boards; if not, we may need the heavy hand of government)
10. Thou shalt watch out for ordinary consumer-citizens – predatory financial practice may be controlled by the new Consumer Financial Protection Bureau

Reproduced from Alan Blinder (2013) p. 433.

Sebastian Faulks, *A Week in December*

In his novel, Sebastian Faulks describes the modern financial world through the musings of Vanessa, the wife of hedge fund manager John Veals, as she tries to understand why he is so well suited to it:

> The essential change seemed to her quite simple: bankers had detached their activities from the real world. Instead of being a 'service' industry – helping companies who had a function in the life of their society – banking became a closed system. Profit was no longer related to growth or increase, but became self-sustaining; and in this semi-virtual world, the amount of money to be made by financiers also became unhitched from normal logic.
>
> It followed, Virginia thought, that the people who could flourish here must themselves be, in some profound and personal way, detached. They could have no qualms about the effects of what they did; no cares for the collateral impact – although, to do them justice, they did take precautions to minimize the possibility of any contact with reality; indeed the joy of the new products was exactly their magical self-sufficiency, the way they appeared to eliminate the risk of any final reckoning. However, it remained necessary for these people to have – or to develop very quickly – a very limited sense of 'the other'; a kind of functional autism was the ideal state of mind.
>
> And in addition to this, there must be a passionate faith: they had to believe that theirs was the true system and that earlier beliefs had been heretical. Where there were doubts, they had to be excised; where there were qualifications, they needed to be cauterized. A breed of fanatic was born...
>
> Some people thought the crux of it was the invention of some credit derivative products by a few

> people at J.P. Morgan, but in fact... the key was that society as a whole in London and New York had so lost its bearings that it was prepared to believe, with these analysts, that cause and effect could be uncoupled. To her this social change, the result of decades of assault on long-accepted norms, was far more interesting than the quasi-autistic intellects of the people, like John, who worked in the new finance.
>
> ...
>
> And somehow money had become the only thing that mattered. When had this happened? When had educated people stopped looking down on money and its acquisition? When had the civilized man stopped viewing money as a means to various enjoyable ends and started to view it as the end itself? When had respectable people given themselves over full-time to counting zeroes?

Reproduced from Sebastian Faulks (2009) pp. 102-103 and 362.

Chapter 3

Economic Progress and Its Discontents

"Possessions, actual or virtual, are indeed necessary to life, but as they increase, their marginal significance to life declines, and the danger arises of sacrificing life to them instead of supporting it on them."
Philip Wicksteed

"Progress threatens to nullify the very goal it is supposed to realize – the idea of man."
Max Horkheimer

"The history of ideas describes how ideas evolve. No one controls the evolution. Change is more organic. Ideas emerge from a variety of sources."
Joseph Stiglitz

From Philosophy to Science
The Rise of Abstraction
What is Self-Interest?
Consumption as the Purpose of Life
Nature Sacrificed
Dehumanized Society
Romanticism Revisited
Happiness is More than Measurement
What Progress Awaits Us?

~~~

In the last chapter, we saw how financialization of the economy through theory and innovation, along with an obsession with money accumulation, helped turn finance away from a constructive purpose to a destructive one. In this chapter, we examine the evolution of economic thinking and its reduction of human motivation to the simple pursuit of wealth. This abstraction of economics and its focus on mathematics and modelling contributed to the divorce of economics from its original purpose of serving the human being. The emphasis in society on monetary wealth, represented through excessive consumption along with a misuse of technological advance, has in fact reduced human dignity and wellbeing. This manifests itself in a collapse of ethical values, rising unhappiness and a detrimental impact on nature.

~~~

From Philosophy to Science

Economics flowed initially from philosophical inquiry, in exploration of how people can best manage their material needs. The concern was for human wellbeing. Classical Greek civilization developed philosophy and mathematics. According to Aristotle, the height of Greek civilization came around 500 BCE with Thales, who first devised the idea that the world can be understood via complex systems that could be reduced to simple principles and explained without resorting to mythical or theological explanations.[1] The first mathematical formulation of a law of nature dated to Pythagoras in the 6th century BCE, paving the way for physics, geometry, algebra and science in general. While the progress of scientific discovery continued, it was not until Galileo discovered the telescope in 1600, thereby consolidating Copernicus's hypothesis formulated a century earlier that the earth was not the centre of the universe, that Modernity 'arrived'. This led on to the Enlightenment and the giving of precedence to science by the 18th century.[2] Since then, science has dominated and has greatly advanced human welfare.

The Enlightenment, an intellectual movement to reform society, stood in opposition to the perceived abuse and intolerance of Church and State in Europe. Rational thought came to fill the void left by the decline in religion and moral consensus, originating in Martin Luther's protest and the Reformation in the 16th century. The absolute power of the Church, which had prevailed until then in Western society, was called into question. A new ideology was introduced; it allowed that reason can uncover, through science, the rules behind the apparent chaos of the human and material world, and hence the rules of natural religion, natural morality and natural law.

As empiricists, leading thinkers accepted that the scientific method of observation and deduction should be applied to human affairs. In economics, this was achieved through mathematics. Quesnay, the economist and physician, who compared the economy to the human body and the flow of money to that of blood, as Franciscan monks in the Middle Ages had before him, devised in 1758 a *tableau économique*,[3] seen as a precursor to econometrics. With the advance of science in Modernity, the quantitative approach came to the fore.

The Enlightenment was the Age of Reason and Science. However, it also witnessed the flowering of humanistic ideals which define Modernity and which remain the foundation of the state in our times: liberty, equality, fraternity and the right to happiness. Such ideas inspired Adam Smith in his economic synthesis and continue today to underpin economic theory, but they have failed to realize their full potential. During the Enlightenment, humanistic thinking remained important, even as science advanced. Today science remains dominant, while humanistic thinking has been largely forgotten. The movement of economics towards abstraction, divorced from philosophical and humanistic considerations, reached its full embodiment in the 20th century.

The Rise of Abstraction

Utilitarianism represented an attempt to keep humanistic ideals alive and relevant within the science of economics. In the 19th century, the concept of happiness figured prominently in social thought and influenced economics and government policy. Jeremy Bentham had introduced the theory of utilitarianism, the principle of 'utility of pleasure' and 'the greatest happiness for the greatest number'.[4] He believed that human motivation is 'hedonic', i.e. to avoid pain and to maximize pleasure and that human action, including economic activity, stems from it. He proposed a scientific and quantitative approach to measure happiness via the 'felicific calculus',[5] based on a formulated algorithm giving rise to units of pleasure.

The economist John Stuart Mill was an early disciple of Bentham, but subsequently followed his own path. His belief in the merits of property is propounded in his treatise, *On Liberty*. Since prosperity was thought to guarantee independence and freedom, it followed naturally that humans would pursue wealth as a step towards happiness. While not coining the term *homo oeconomicus*,[6] Mill advanced the idea of 'economic man' in his book, *The Principles of Political Economy*, which dominated economic thought for several decades in the second half of the 19th century. He writes: "Political economy does not treat… the whole conduct of man in society. It is concerned with him solely as a being who desires to possess wealth, and who is capable of judging that end… It makes entire abstraction of every other human passion or motive."[7]

Economic man came to be seen as the standard economic agent and rational wealth maximizer, as the model of motivation. This assumption led to the eventual and pervasive perception in the 19th century that the purpose of life was the possession and maximization of wealth, and this continues today. This premise has become the basis for organizing society and grounds for political policy and action. Mill argues that such a simplifying assumption of motivation is necessary "because this is the mode in which science must necessarily proceed".[8]

While the idea of the utility of pleasure subsequently lost ground, that of economic utility remained and helped transform economics fully into a science through the derivation of economic law from a single fundamental "law of human nature", that of rational calculation to maximize economic utility.[9] In the eyes of many, this law allows us to understand the whole of economic reality. Like Mill, both Alfred Marshall and John Maynard Keynes acknowledge that economics leaves out many other human motivations, but maintain that this is unavoidable, as it would be impractical otherwise.

The metaphor of the map is sometimes used in economics to defend the simplification of assumptions. The logic is that the map of a mountain is imperfect, but useful because of its simplification. Likewise in economics, if everything were considered, it would be useless as a tool. A good economic model underlines what is important and keeps the most relevant elements and discards the rest, including the qualitative, as noise. In fact, Marshall argues that although custom appears to be the underlying cause of economic activity, economics owes its continued existence to efficiency.[10] As the driving force in economics, efficiency requires simplification in approach and process. Because resources are limited, economic efficiency allows society to meet its material needs and to survive, with production maximized and waste minimized.[11]

A development in economics that advances efficiency is 'instrumentality', which establishes what economic preferences are, as expressed through choice, and how objectives can be attained within a given set of conditions.[12] It is not necessary to question or discuss the process of making the choice or its motivation, but simply to consider the outcome or manifested preference, a given based on observed behaviour. Economics as science is concerned simply with the determination of preference as goal, leading to action, in order to attain that goal. Over time, economists increasingly declared economics to be independent of the study of human motivation and became interested simply in facts of preference or choice. Economics thus became explicitly tautological and irrefutable – people choose what they want and what they want is defined by what they choose; the theory says no more and thus cannot be falsified.[13]

The late 19th and early 20th century was a fruitful time for the development of theory and principles to explain economic behaviour. This coincided with the start of mass production and consumption, which required that *efficiency* be developed and consumer behaviour understood. Economics thus became the science of managing and optimizing scarce resources through efficiency, with minimization of input and maximization of utility and output, and competition providing the determining and balancing force. The maximization of profit is seen in the same light of efficiency.

Developments in economic history helped advance our material welfare, but at the same time they transformed economics into what became first and foremost a model of mathematical efficiency and began to divorce it from considered discussion of the total human condition. Efficiency came to be seen as a crucial social goal because it allows greater participation, either by making it possible for an economic good to be shared among more people or by allowing the size of the economic pie to increase, thereby allowing everyone a larger slice.[14] National income was established as a gauge of national welfare and government policy focused on increasing income. Human activity was reduced to mathematical calculation and what mattered was quantitative consequence.

The problem with this approach is not *per se* in mathematics, which plays a useful role, but in the disregard for complex human issues in economics. Improving national welfare is indeed a worthy goal, but increasing national income proved not to benefit all, as inequality expanded. This is further complicated by the detrimental impact of growth on nature. And the human being seeks more in life than simply monetary wealth. The human condition became impoverished in the process.

Abstraction in economics gained further ground in the second half of the 20th century. It was thought necessary to resolve complex issues in an increasingly extended society. Milton Friedman proposed that behavioural assumptions about individuals need not be accurate, as long as aggregate data, such as Price and Quantity, behaved as if they were. [15] He argued for the use of econometrics to derive statistical relationships between consumer demand and various empirically measurable factors that influence this demand. Consumer behaviour is explained by breaking it down into its component parts; macroeconomic behaviour is the sum of all individual consumers' behaviour. Since economics was believed not to need a theory of value, but just a theory of price determinism, economics was left primarily to the analysis of price and quantity.[16]

The process of abstraction was furthered by Paul Samuelson, who saw the mathematical function of maximizing output under resource constraints as a simple principle at the heart of all economic problems.[17] He introduced 'revealed preference theory', which developed the link between individual demand functions and preferences, freeing economics completely from the consideration of psychology and basing it simply on observable consumer purchasing behaviour.[18] Samuelson was the first American to receive the Nobel Prize in Economics. His book, *Economics: An Introductory Analysis*, was the textbook of reference for several decades in the second half of the 20th century,[19] just as Mill's had been a century earlier. Samuelson also played a key role in the development of econometrics, or economic modelling, which seeks to verify deductive *a priori* principles that cannot be empirically tested.

Whilst modelling helps in the understanding of economic theory and forecasting, nonetheless, purely deductive reasoning and highly mathematical formulas can divorce theory from the human reality. As noted by Mark Skousen, it can have detrimental effects: "Heuristic model building can be useful in generating best estimates and decent results, but modelling can easily distort reality and lead to damaging results".[20] Even the physicists Stephen Hawking and Leonard Mlodinow recognize that effective theory[21] is only moderately successful: "decisions are often not rational or are based on a defective analysis of the consequences of the choice. That is why the world is in such a mess."[22] Our reality is much more complex than the simplifying process of economic theory allows.

This is not to belittle the important contribution that economics has made to improving our material organization and raising living standards. It is to show how its abstraction has removed the need to consider the total wellbeing of the person, who is at its centre. Since it is not necessary to question the formation of preference or to attribute human motivation to it, there is no need for any discussion of human value. As a result, economics moved further away from its roots in philosophy, where the total wellbeing of the human being is considered. Our society is now organized around *homo oeconomicus,* even in areas outside economics and finance. This deductive view of the person, with wealth accumulation as the overdriving motivation, has damaged society. The mathematics of economics provides an important contribution to understanding how material affairs can be efficiently organized, but this should be accompanied by human consideration.

What is Self-Interest?

What do human beings aspire to? Is it purely material advancement for the self, or more? Defenders of unchallenged free markets have misappropriated Adam Smith's argument of "self-interest"[23] to justify their ideology. Smith writes that landlords in "their natural selfishness and rapacity" to pursue "their own vain and insatiable desires" employ thousands of workers. Thus it is argued that in market operations, it is not necessary to look beyond self-interest. As long as one furthers one's own cause, others will end up benefiting via the invisible hand. For economics, the only assessment of success or failure is material advancement. The success or failure of a market operation is measured in the units of wealth arising from it, and maximization is the goal. We do not question who gets to appropriate the wealth created or whether any detrimental effect results from the operation.

In our economic and financial world, self-interest is understood as simple egoism, fully accepted and in fact seen as an indispensable motivation for competition, which furthers our material lot in life. But if we read Adam Smith carefully, we learn that his concept of self-interest embodies virtue and "self-command". Smith's admiration for the Stoics is voiced in his *Theory of Moral Sentiments* through his conviction of a need "to promote the general order and happiness of the whole".[24] Smith and David Hume, his friend and mentor, believe that a society that is both moral and prosperous is possible and in fact ensures happiness. Establishing a virtuous society requires a systematic understanding of right and wrong. These are not relativist ideas; there are certain absolute truths. For Smith, selfishness and greed are vices; whereas, for many in the financial world, influenced by Ayn Rand, selfishness and greed are seen as virtues,[25] for they promote wealth creation.

In the past generation, during a period of unfettered markets, we have witnessed an ethical collapse. Money and instant gratification have become the underlying motivation driving human action. Until the financial collapse, money was easy and goods were abundant. For some people, this situation has continued despite the crisis. People's worth has been increasingly defined by what they possess materially, rather than what human qualities they exhibit. As materialism gained ground, humanity was degraded. Honesty, trust and compassion have been sacrificed for monetary gain, and avarice, dishonesty and hubris have become accepted traits, entrenched in society, and in fact often seen as beneficial for self-advancement. The person has become increasingly fragmented, perhaps exhibiting caring and cooperative qualities within the family and his immediate circle and community and cold-hearted indifference towards the outside world, and even at times engaging in behaviour that is detrimental to that world.

The cascade of lawsuits and huge fines on banks and the financial sector for breaches of the law, including insider trading, the fixing of Libor, collusion on exchange rates and other predatory market activity provide material for a modern morality tale. These transgressions took place at the very top, amongst the most prestigious financial institutions, those lauded for creating wealth for all. These developments show that the problem is not simply that of certain dishonest individuals, but of a system that has been corrupted and is in desperate need of reform.

The English philosopher, Onora O'Neil, describes our current crisis as primarily one of trust.[26] Joseph Stiglitz writes that "there are often implicit contracts, understandings, norms, which enable society to function well. What makes economic systems work, by and large is trust... In recent years, in failed societies, we see the disastrous consequences for the economy of the breakdown of trust. Because such implicit contracts cannot typically be enforced in court, they can be torn up at will. In the 1990s, essential pieces of the social contract were torn to pieces. And as one firm tore up its contract, bottom-line economics put pressures on others to do so... Competition does not always lead to efficient outcomes: here, it led to a race to the bottom."[27]

Structures of trust between people have become known as 'social capital' because of their importance in both community and economic activity.[28] We have seen that trust is the foundation of money and banking. Trust cannot be legislated or enforced. It can only be integrated into custom through human action and it is indispensable if we are truly to flourish. Our moral decline as described by Vaclav Havel has to be reversed: "The worst thing is that we lived in a contaminated moral environment. We fell morally ill because we got used to saying something different from what we thought. We learned not to believe in anything, to ignore each other, to care only for ourselves. Concepts that define human wealth, such as love, friendship, compassion, humility and forgiveness, lost their depth and dimensions."[29] Until we recover human wealth, we cannot move forward to a better future.

Consumption as the Purpose of Life

Our obsession with consumption has furthered the cause of money and contributed to this decline. Excessive consumption feeds greed, narcissism and a false sense of security that reinforces the ego. The advertising industry uses psychological manipulation to encourage consumption. Techniques developed by psychologists, including Edward Bernays,[30] a nephew of Sigmund Freud, and Ernest Dichter,[31] also from Vienna, began the exploitation of mass psychology to promote consumption. This prepared the ground in the first half of the 20th century for spin and manipulation through advertising. Dichter acknowledged that consumption often did not have anything to do with the product itself, but with "illusionary brand images".[32]

Following World War II, with the availability of goods outstripping demand, it was necessary to encourage purchases to keep the production machine going. Also, consumer culture was seen as a defence against socialism and crucial for national security. Dichter writes that "the needs and wants of people have to be continuously stirred up", so that they will continue to work hard to buy what they desire.[33] Dichter also contributed to the development of consumer debt by convincing banks to offer overdrafts to allow purchases despite inadequate funds. Thus began the mass consumption and debt cycles in the second half of the 20th century, first in the United States and then copied worldwide.

Consumption is promoted as the purpose of life and serves as the major engine of our economy. Because we need money for consumption, money is perceived as the goal in life. However, money serves as a means to meet our material needs; it is not our human purpose.[34] In *Modern Culture*, the philosopher Roger Scruton writes about "the advent of the consumer society, when all the channels of social life are devoted to consumption".[35] However, he notes that "the consumer's goals are perpetually recurring illusions, which vanish at the very moment they loom into view". Thus, we are surrounded by "a world of consumables, to be devoured by relentless and ultimately purposeless appetites". This has contributed to a sense of emptiness in our times, to a lack of meaning in life, often leading to alienation, anxiety and unhappiness.

Consumption had a relatively benign beginning. At the start of the 20th century, the economist Thorstein Veblen first wrote about the expanding desire for goods and comfort. Advances in industrial efficiency allowed for progress beyond a bare livelihood satisfying basic needs for survival. The accumulation of goods made life more comfortable, but it also began to serve as evidence of wealth or power, encouraging ideas of status and esteem. Veblen introduced into the vernacular the term "conspicuous consumption".[36] People were fascinated by the lifestyle of the wealthy. Imitating them provided an escape from drudgery in the early days of industry. In a similar vein, we are fascinated by the lifestyle of celebrities and the super-rich today. How do we define *success* and what elicits our admiration? The way we perceive success influences the way we behave and shape society.

In our world, success is still defined in most cases by monetary gain or pecuniary achievement. Veblen writes: "the motive that lies at the root of ownership is emulation... The possession of wealth confers honour; it is an invidious distinction."[37] Whereas the justification of wealth-creation in Adam Smith's time was to ensure liberty, today its purpose appears to be primarily to permit ever-increasing consumption in the developed world. Until we adopt another vision of success and use it as the bar against which to measure human progress, we will remain ensnared in the consumption machine. Scruton points out that monetary success allows for fantasy, but he alerts us to the risk that in such a world "humanity itself may be profaned, and will be profaned when fantasy takes charge of human dealings... [and] erodes all higher feelings".[38]

Scruton also distinguishes between 'fantasy' and 'imagination': "Both... concern unrealities; but while the unrealities of fantasy penetrate and pollute the world, those of the imagination exist in a world of their own, in which we wander freely and in full knowledge of the really real".[39] While fantasy is an escape, imagination helps us advance to a better reality. It creates and constructs. In order to allow progress to serve us, we need to remember the original purpose of money and imagine a way to use it well.

Nature Sacrificed

Concurrent with our economic and financial crisis, the environmental crisis, exacerbated by wasteful consumption, is increasingly visible and acknowledged. Extraction of resources for production at minimal cost, so as to allow for maximal consumption, has led to unprecedented damage to the environment: pollution, resource depletion and climate change. Our economic paradigm does not attach any value to nature, other than as a resource for exploitation. We do not factor in the cost of the consequent damage. In economic parlance, we do not consider externalities. For example, in our use of energy, we do not account for carbon emissions that contribute to the risk of climate change, with all its implicit costs. Mindless of the full economic cost, we deplete resources and cause environmental havoc by our actions, the ramifications of which extend beyond immediate economic impact to the disintegration of nature.

We are changing the earth's ecological balance, from oceans to glaciers, rivers, water tables, topsoil and animal and plant species. Optimists feel we are advanced enough scientifically and technologically to redress the balance, for we have become a geological force. But what is the potential price to nature and to humanity? We cannot assess human action only through numbers, whether expressed as cost, profit or growth. British mathematician and philosopher Alfred North Whitehead calls the obsession with measurement "the fallacy of misplaced concreteness".[40] Because something is concrete, we have full faith in it, but resolving the environmental crisis demands more than economics and science; it demands full human engagement. Unless we see ourselves as part of nature in all its awe and magnificence, nature will continue to be sacrificed.

Al Gore, in his book *The Future*, writes that our focus on growth, compounded by globalization and population expansion, has contributed to what biologists refer to as the Sixth Great Extinction. Unlike the previous five, this is "precipitated entirely by man" according to the distinguished biologist E.O. Wilson.[41] We are at a potentially dangerous "planetary scale tipping point".[42] The number of people on the planet, the power of technology and globalization collide with resource limits, and yet growth continues to be the principal and overriding objective. Gore writes that the primary way of measuring economic growth – the gross domestic product or GDP – is based on "absurd calculations that completely exclude any consideration of the distribution of income, the relentless depletion of essential resources, and the reckless spewing of prodigious quantities of harmful waste into the atmosphere, oceans, rivers, soil and biosphere".[43]

Gore's comment reminds us of Robert F. Kennedy's remarks at the University of Kansas in 1968, at a time when it was still possible to *dream* of things beyond money: "Yet the gross national product does not allow for the health of our children, the quality of their education or the joy of their play. It does not include the beauty of our poetry or the strength of our marriages, the intelligence of our public debate or the integrity of our public officials. It measures neither our wit nor our courage, neither our wisdom nor our learning, neither our compassion nor our devotion to our country, it measures everything in short, except that which makes life worthwhile."[44]

Naomi Klein goes further in condemning human action that is detrimental to nature. In fact, she places our economic system in a clash with climate protection and calls this a 'battle of world-views',[45] as fault lines have been exposed in free market ideology and organization. She explains that the defence of free trade and the profit-seeking motives that drive corporations and investors have often been directly at odds with the environmentally friendly industrial action that is needed. Addressing climate risk would include long-term planning, taxation, public spending, tough regulation of business, and community involvement, as well as a different attitude towards investment and consumption. Klein maintains that appropriate climate action can be used to transform the economy into a sustainable one, creating new jobs in the construction of new systems and business models in energy creation and transportation, while avoiding the dangers inherent in certain geo-engineering responses. The urgency of the problem is contributing to cultural transformation. She says that human engagement will not only help restore nature, but lead to more humane and fulfilling lifestyles.

What does economic growth indeed serve? Can we continue to pursue it blindly? Or is it time to re-evaluate the original purpose of the economy in light of current conditions and constraints? It is vital that we have a deep and communal reflection on this question – a reflection that will lead to proper action. Environmental responsibility is a key part of this dialogue, and inspired leadership is required. We can view this as a matter of justice or proportionality, the key virtue allowing for the smooth functioning of an economy, as discussed by Aristotle. It is justice towards nature and future generations, with whom we have to share our earth; and it is stewardship as discussed by Locke. We cannot expropriate resources in a way that jeopardizes the earth and mankind's future. We recall Aristotle's definition of the economy as management of the home. The earth is our home. We are linked to nature and are a part of it. In fact, we are inseparable from it. By sacrificing nature, we sacrifice ourselves. We are more at risk than the planet. With environmental disruption, the earth will survive in an altered state, but we may not escape disaster.

Dehumanized Society

Abstraction in economics, the commercialization of life, the destruction of nature, and nefarious elements in the world of finance have all contributed to a society that is dehumanized. Technology threatens to bring us further down that path to a point where the situation is irremediable. Reclaiming our humanity is a long path. Firstly, education needs reform and the humanities must regain the ground they have lost to science. In The Two Cultures, C.P. Snow discusses literary and scientific cultures, divided by an "ocean" or a "gulf of mutual incomprehension". Snow believes that specialization of education is to blame for this schism.[46] The literary deals with human concerns, while the scientific is preoccupied with efficiency, and both follow separate paths. Before Snow, Veblen saw that the terms of standardization, validity and finality as used in modern technology and science are always impersonal and not terms of humanity and nature.[47] Veblen describes the dominant note of technology as that of a barbaric competitive expediency.

Technology has advanced our material condition, but the human being is paying a high price. Max Horkheimer, writing in the first half of the 20th century, discusses the process of dehumanization in *Eclipse of Reason.*[48] He laments the decline in imagination and independent judgement and ability to resist the growing apparatus of mass manipulation. We are no longer capable of passing judgement on our way of life. Reason has lost its potency as a Socratic guiding principle, as the "supreme arbiter... the creative force behind the ideas and things to which we should devote our lives". Ideas have become automatic and instrumental; they have lost depth of meaning, as the functional gains ascendance.

With the emergence of industrial society, Horkheimer notes that human activity is transformed into commodities. Even leisure finds its justification in the opportunities it creates for commerce and industry. And philosophy has embarked on a pragmatic course with the determining of practical action through the logic of probability, rather than providing insight. The search for truth and meaningful purpose has lost its appeal. "Pragmatism reflects a society that has no time to remember and meditate". We have transformed the world into facts and things, and fail to connect this with the social process and with human purpose. As Horkheimer describes, it is not technology *per se* that is the culprit, but our idealization of it: "Such an ideology tends to supplant the humanistic foundation of the very civilization it seeks to glorify".

In *The Technological Society*, a book published twenty years later in 1964, Jacques Ellul describes the tragedy of a civilization dominated by what he calls technique, "the totality of methods rationally arrived at and having absolute efficiency (for a given stage of development) in every field of human activity".[49] It goes beyond industrial life to affect all aspects of human life. Technique has integrated the machine into society and everything else. Ellul writes that "when technique enters into every area of life, including the human, it ceases to be external to man and becomes his very substance", leading to the standardization and rationalization of social, economic and administrative life. This creates 'impersonality' and leaves no room for inspiration, ingenuity or intelligence to resolve difficulties. All our human aspirations and tragedies are relegated to mechanical problems, which are to be solved not through the spirit but through engineering and mathematics.

Ellul traces the flowering of technique to the optimism experienced in the 18th century, which created a favourable climate for the rise of technical applications. "There was... a certain delight in life, which was greatly increased by the improvement of living conditions in nearly all classes... All these helped persuade Europeans that progress could only be achieved by the exploitation of natural resources and the application of scientific discoveries... They believed that happiness and justice could result from their investigations; and it is here that the myth of progress had its beginning." It was a period of hope and full faith in scientific and technical progress, which responded to the needs of an expanding population in the 18th century: "drawn by self-interest (the ideal of comfort, for instance), the masses went over to the side of technique; society was converted".

Modern technique assumes "the one best way", thus eliminating personal choice. "Technique reigns alone, a blind force and more clear-sighted than the best human intelligence." The most disturbing aspect highlighted by Ellul is that technique never observes the distinction between moral and immoral use, for it creates its independent technical morality. Necessity justifies the technical universe, which invades all economic activity. As pointed out by Keynes in his *General Theory,* technical progress is an indispensable factor in the economy and central to the theory of investment. If technical arrest were to occur in the economy, it would represent a regression, with resultant deep crisis. Thus, we appear to be gripped in a Faustian bargain.

Do advances in technology reduce the capacity of the public to influence its course? Ellul writes that "technique always creates a kind of secret society, a closed fraternity of its practitioners... [and] economic life, not in its content but in its direction, will henceforth entirely elude popular control". He argues that the further economic technique develops, the more it makes real the abstract conception of 'economic man', with the devaluation of all human activities and tendencies other than the economic, leading to the whole of human life becoming a function of economic technique. Half a century after Ellul wrote his book, the situation persists and is compounded by the dizzying pace of technological advance, with its consequent transformation of society[50] the organization of the economy[51] and employment.[52]

In our time, Jaron Lanier[53], a computer scientist and pioneer of virtual reality, writes about the risk of technology overtaking our destiny. He describes the exploitation of behaviour by technology through the manipulation of our cognitive experience. He highlights how crucial it is to defend against the design of such direct manipulations and proposes that technology experts and society enter into talks about the human relationship with technology. He discusses the risk of technological advance in negating human understanding, as we judge success in terms of how well data is manipulated in the 'cloud' rather than in terms of sound principles and judgement. He stresses the importance of reflection, to take time to hear the 'inner voice'.[54] He acknowledges that the person is more complex than a computer can design and writes: "What is a person? If I knew the answer to that, I might be able to program an artificial person in a computer. But I can't. Being a person is not a pat formula, but a quest, a mystery, a leap of faith."[55] As a result, we have a chance to resist technological takeover, but this demands reflection and ethical action.

Romanticism Revisited

We need to question certain aspects of our 'progress'. Revisiting the English Romantic Movement of the 19th century might help us understand some of the issues we face, even if our times are very different. This movement arose in reaction to the rapid transformation of England into an industrial society, when the discrepancy between economic and human progress became striking. Richard Bronk writes that Romanticism in fact represented a revolution in thought against the cold reductionist rationalism following the Enlightenment.[56] Among the major thinkers of that time, Thomas Carlyle, who had described economics as a 'dismal science', was convinced that grave moral and social consequences flowed from understanding society as a machine; that it would force us into an "unwise mode of viewing Nature" (including humans).[57] In fact, we realize now how prescient he was.

Carlyle was alarmed by the pervasive power of the mechanistic metaphors used by rationalist thinkers, particularly the 'Machine of Society', with humans as cogs. Our analysis, moral beliefs and vision of the human being began to be structured by mechanism. In his *Last Words,* Carlyle laments "the conversion of Human Commerce and Enterprise... into ardent Gambling... Let us expect to see noble commerce then become yearly more and more ignoble, blackguard, and accursed."[58] Despite the intensely moralistic tone to which we are no longer accustomed, Carlyle's prophetic words are worth pondering, for they point to a continued, dark and deepening reality.

John Ruskin likewise saw danger in reducing human motivation to the merely economic. In his diatribe against John Stuart Mill's political economy,[59] he notes that in human social affairs, disturbing causes "operate, not mathematically, but chemically", that is, they alter the essence of what is going on.[60] For Ruskin, Mill failed to understand this or appreciate the central importance of wider motivational factors, such as loyalty and the pursuit of excellence, in commerce and economic behaviour. He derides Mill's economics as an abstract "science deficient only in applicability".[61]

However, Mill was actually a complex thinker.[62] Even if he felt that, of necessity, economic principles had to be simplified in order to be useful, he was also the economist who later discovered the force of love, of focusing on another's wellbeing rather than one's own, which is the ultimate manifestation of loyalty and pursuit of excellence. We shall explore this humanistic aspect of Mill later. Ruskin and Mill were actually similarly inspired by the higher realms of human sentiment but, whereas Mill felt first the need to compromise in order to advance the cause of economics as science, Ruskin highlighted the danger of doing so.

Thomas Coleridge and the Lake poets were also great critics of political economy and the utilitarianism associated with it. They felt that happiness could not be simply treated as the maximization of pleasure and the minimization of pain, for the human condition is much more creative and complex. While Coleridge was opposed to political economy, he was not hostile to commerce or trade.[63] He argued that it is not the spirit of barter *per se* that causes problems, but the lack of suitable "correctives of the commercial spirit" in the form of religion and respect for tradition that can act as a "countercharm to the sorcery of wealth".[64] Coleridge focused on culture, the national character, and viewed education as the formation of human society. He had a holistic view.

Another poet Percy Bysshe Shelley attacked the limitations of political economy, science and utilitarianism: "the selfish and calculating principle" which divorced people from "the creative faculty".[65] Thus, as Bronk illustrates, we see in the poets and thinkers of the Romantic period a concern about the detrimental impact that the economy can have on humans, if its development is not properly steered with full consideration for the manifold aspects of the human being and human aspiration.

Happiness is More than Measurement

This leads us to a central discussion today: the desire for happiness and its elusiveness, debated even during prosperous times. This dilemma has been aggravated by the economic and financial crisis, as stress and anxiety keep us from attaining happiness. The link between inequality and stress is acknowledged, as people find it difficult to make ends meet or to keep pace with the pervasive consumption machine. Our tendency to assess the worth of a person in terms of their wealth enhances status anxiety and provokes depression, as well as insecurity and narcissism.[66] This condition reduces the trust that we have in one another. It contributes to a decline in social capital, or the sum total of people's involvement in community life.[67] People feel isolated and alienated and thus further removed from happiness. The debate around these issues has led governments to examine what promotes wellbeing and to expand measurement beyond simple economic output. In this way, the issue of happiness has returned to economics.

While he was President, Nicolas Sarkozy, dissatisfied with GDP as a gauge of the wellbeing of the French people, asked whether other considerations could be included. As a result, Joseph Stiglitz and Amartya Sen, with participation by other academics, published the *Report by the Commission on the Measurement of Economic Performance and Social Progress*. This study seeks "to identify the limits of GDP as an indicator of economic performance and social progress, including the problems with its measurement [and] to consider what additional information might be required for the production of more relevant indicators of social progress".[68] It recommends a focus on income and consumption as a measurement of wellbeing rather than production; giving more prominence to distribution; and broadening measures to include non-market activities and the quality of life, with consideration of the environment and sustainability – all issues of importance, but in some ways contradictory. How do we reconcile consumption with protection of the environment and sustainability? Clearly this will require a different approach to production and consumption than the wasteful one we have today and in fact provides an avenue for creativity.

In a similar vein, Prime Minister David Cameron requested the Office of National Statistics in 2010 to establish a "national wellbeing index".[69] Richard Layard, economist and expert on the study of happiness, advised. Following consultations, a questionnaire was devised to incorporate matters seen to influence wellbeing and designed to help policy-makers to understand what conditions affect people's happiness or cause misery. The method uses surveys; according to Layard: "If we want to measure the quality of life, it must be based on how people feel".[70] The approach is inspired by Bentham's felicific calculus, a measure of the maximization of happiness, and it continues within the *scientific* realm. Layard desires human betterment and believes, as Bentham did, that the best society is one where the citizens are happiest.[71] With this I agree. However, although such measurement plays a useful role in focusing government's attention on what may be vital for society other than output, it is but one of many steps in necessary policy reform. Is human aspiration not deeper than any measurement can fathom? Can the discussion of happiness rest solely in the statistical arena, to be resolved through cost-benefit analysis, without calling forth a philosophical debate and entering the *subjective* realm?

Bruno Frey argues in *Happiness: A Revolution in Economics* that research into happiness is useful for economic policy. He highlights the relationship between income and happiness, important in relative and not absolute terms, for desires tend to be insatiable. A state of happiness is attained when one is improved in condition compared to the other. At the same time, unemployment causes unhappiness as does inflation, because income is then either not forthcoming or else reduced in real terms by rising prices. Another culprit is inequality, as one feels diminished in status and circumstance. Frey points out that the impact of inequality is greater in Europe than the United States, perhaps because of the American illusion of social mobility, which has since been disproved,[72] and the discussion around inequality has gained centre stage worldwide. Frey discusses even marriage as an economic model with specialization and division of labour and commitment to a mutually rewarding exchange; and he determines that married people are happier. Thus, economic decisions are seen as useful in guiding even our private realm. The focus on markets in all realms is based on the assumption that money is the prime mover in human behaviour and a major source of happiness.

In contrast, the psychologist Daniel Gilbert writes that "wealth does not necessarily make people happy, but it serves the needs of the economy, which serves the needs of a stable society, which serves as a network for the propagation of delusional beliefs about happiness and wealth".[73] This is part of our cultural view: "We are nodes in a social network that arises and falls by a logic of its own".[74] The discussion of happiness is intertwined with our economic debate. We are led to believe that we are happy by being better off than others. However, with happiness, we are not in a competitive realm. It is not as simple a matter as whether we earn above US$75,000,[75] or where we are placed in our earning power, compared to others. We can observe that economic deprivation brings unhappiness, but can we deduce that financial abundance alone engenders happiness? Such a perspective is influenced by the advertising world, which seeks to manipulate us into believing that pleasure comes from consumption, which enhances status, and that pleasure equates to happiness.

In *Exploring Happiness,* Sisella Bok[76] discusses today's idea of happiness, illustrated by Freud's narrowly hedonic view that pleasure alone could bring spurts of happiness. For Freud, all hope of long-term happiness is based on delusion and bound to be frustrated; short-term pleasure is all one can hope for. In 1971 two psychologists, Philip Brickman and Donald Campbell, coined the term 'hedonic treadmill' to suggest that people respond only briefly to the ups and downs of pleasure and then return to a neutral state. Are we really condemned to fleeting moments of frustrated happiness and the anxiety of elusive pursuit?

Is happiness just the maximization of pleasure and avoidance of pain, espoused by Jeremy Bentham as his two "sovereign masters"[77] and advocated by Richard Layard, who defines happiness as "feeling good – enjoying life and wanting the feeling to be maintained"?[78] Layard, though, does not rest his argument simply on "feeling good". He explores what would make for a happy society and includes the importance of security, trust, engagement and cooperation and the promotion of human qualities other than status, as worthy of admiration and respect. He says that happiness depends on the inner life as much as on outer circumstances. The implication, missed by the many constructors of new Happiness Indices, is that understanding what we can measure in the aggregate is bound to be inadequate.

What Progress Awaits Us?

We are living through a major crisis and we are at a critical juncture in history. Economic and financial sophistication has not served us well. Computer technology and algorithms, devised by physicists for financial trading and speculation, have brought the financial and economic spheres further and further away from the human being who is at the centre of economic activity and bear their share of blame for leading us to the financial crisis. There is an increasing acknowledgement that something needs addressing at a much deeper level than economic and financial theory can offer, and economists are perplexed as to where the solution may lie.[79]

In their book on economic history, Ernesto Screpanti and Stefano Zamagni write that "the evolution of economic ideas proceeds in jumps, through a succession of epochs of revolution and consolidation: of language confusion and 'classical' periods".[80] Are we currently undergoing a period of cacophonous change, where fruitful work may be taking place "underground, like a river of limestone" and where a clear strand in new thinking will eventually emerge, as with this river? New facts emerging in the course of economic evolution modify political ideas about what is important to society. For Screpanti and Zamagni, "society as a whole decrees the importance of the problems to be studied, establishes the directions in which solutions should be sought, and, ultimately, decides which theories are correct".[81] In this way, we can influence our future.

A central consideration in this debate is the trade-off between the immediate and the long term. In economic and financial management, as in our dealings with nature, we favour immediate gratification, without recognizing the price this may entail. In his book, *The Theory of Interest,* Irving Fisher writes: "Society may add to or subtract from its income stream at will at any period, present or future. But beyond a certain point every addition at one period must be at the cost of a subtraction at some other period." If we take from future income, we decrease our future wealth. He writes that "the rate of return over cost is thus a social phenomenon of great significance. There are two and only two ways in which society may affect the present cost and the future return. It may affect the present cost by exerting more present labour or by abstracting more from present consumption; and it may realize the future return over that cost either in the form of more future consumption or of less future toil."[82] In order to attain long-term benefit, Fisher writes of *sacrifice*, a term that many people shun, for immediate gratification is what we tend to pursue. As a consequence of all this, the merit of saving and investment, of providing for a better future, as discussed earlier, cannot be ignored.

Economists use the polarity of cultural perspectives (set against personal opinion and desire), as well as our extended and anonymous world (as opposed to a smaller concrete and personal world), to defend abstraction in economics. However, as we have discussed, human wellbeing has been impoverished by this. In recent years, behavioural economics has gained ground. Daniel Kahneman, a psychologist awarded the Nobel Prize in Economics in 2002, has debunked the idea that humans behave rationally, a key assumption in standard economic and financial theory.[83] He argues that people are not fully rational or completely selfish, that tastes are unstable. He points to systematic errors or biases of intuition, showing how difficult it is to arrive at any precise discussion or agreement when objective reality eludes us. Therefore, although psychology is being reintroduced into the study of economics, the complexity of human behaviour renders the task difficult.

We need to go further in order to bring about an economic approach that is concerned with the total human condition. Keynes notes that an economist must be "mathematician, historian, statesman and philosopher".[84] Pope Francis highlights this concern for the human being in his 2014 message to the political and business community at the World Economic Forum in Davos.[85] He emphasizes "human dignity" and the "common good" through promotion of an inclusive approach and elimination of a wasteful attitude towards resources. He appeals to "a renewed, profound and broadened sense of responsibility", which demands more than economic growth and a simple welfare mentality. This requires "a transcendent vision of the person"[86] and "economic and financial activity within the horizon of an ethical approach which is truly humane... to ensure that humanity is served by wealth and not ruled by it". Humanistic considerations must perforce return to the economic debate, in order to maintain liberty, reinforce equality, reintroduce fraternity and understand true happiness. Within this discourse, virtue is indispensable as restraint and love as illumination and motivation. A 'New Enlightenment' is in order.

There is reason to be hopeful, as new economic thinking increasingly incorporates consideration not only for the person, but also for nature. We live in a world of finite and declining resources. Some economists have argued that resources are infinite, because intellectual and technological advances continually extend the frontier. But Nicholas Georgescu-Roegen exposes the myth that we will always find a substitute for a resource which has become scarce and increase the productivity of any kind of energy and material; and that if we run out of some resources, we will think up something else.[87] This supposition places unwarranted confidence in the intellectual capacity of humans and the technological capacity of machines.

As well as the human limitations we have witnessed in the financial sphere, we have seen detrimental effects from economic advance, such as the threat to nature. According to the basic law of thermodynamics, Georgescu-Roegen argues that humankind's dowry is finite. We have to find a way to use it well. A core principle in economics is 'scarcity'. There is a trade-off required in choice, and more of a good thing often means less of another within the material realm. But the good things that we need to consider are not only material ones, but those that have an impact on our humanity. In the non-material realm, the same principle of scarcity does not apply, as we shall explore.

In an interview in 1994, José Saramago, the Portuguese Nobel Laureate in Literature, said: "If humans are incapable of organizing a world economy to satisfy the needs of a world that is starving of hunger and much else, what humanity is this? We fill our palate with the word 'humanity', but I believe we have not arrived at this; we are not human beings... And as long as the consciousness of people is not awakened, this will remain. For much that we do, it is done to maintain us in lack of will, in weakness of purpose, to diminish our capacity for civic action."[88]

Seventy years earlier, in 1925, another Nobel Laureate, the Indian poet Rabindranath Tagore discussed the consequences of human action. He described William Wordsworth as becoming "sad when he saw what man had done to man" for "men are ever the greatest enemy of man". He questioned whether Europe "may miss greatness in spite of success" for "everywhere we are faced with... progress towards inhospitable ugliness". Tagore aspired to love, for it "is the highest human truth, and truth gives the fullness of life" and aspired also to the "Unity of Man".[89] We are facing similar challenges today.

Part II: The Person: Love and Virtue

Chapter 4

Recovering Virtue and the Common Good

"The primary support of civil society, the most important of all, is love for the public good."
Antonio Genovesi

"No society can surely be flourishing and happy, of which the far greater part of the members are poor and miserable."
Adam Smith

"An exuberant blossoming of ethical creativity seems to be the most desperate need of humanity today."
Pitirim Sorokin

What is the Starting Point?
Ideas, Language and Custom: The Person
Recovering Virtue
Restoring Justice
Virtue and Dignity in Markets
The Common Good

~~~

In the preceding chapters, we saw how the reduction of human motivation to the pursuit of wealth has led to an economic model that does not serve the human being well and to abuse in finance. The focus has been on abstract theory and instrumentality, and not underlying human considerations. Theory has been deficient in serving the human being. How does our view of the person affect the way we organize society? Should the social contract be based on fear or trust? On manipulation and deceit, or consideration? Is justice purely governed by law or also by good action? What is necessary in order to attain forms of economic and financial organization that will provide full prosperity and serve the common good? Is it possible without recovering virtue?

~~~

What is the Starting Point?

Central to any concept of a social order, including the economic and financial, are the underlying assumptions we hold about the nature of the human being, and this influences the way we organize ourselves. Are people inherently evil or good, egoistical or compassionate? Is human behaviour determined by nature or culture? Our modern forms of social organization stem from an overwhelming bias towards assuming an egoistic human appetite and personal ambition that allows us to engage in deception. Most people agree that a positive view would be desirable, but think it unrealistic and unattainable. Some even think a positive view is contrary to human nature. But is it? Our view of the human being does influence the historical outcome. Should we maintain a pessimistic view? Will this not take us further along a path of decline?

The roots of this pessimism are old. Power has long been associated with competitive struggle. This perception has played an important part in influencing social, economic and financial behaviour. We can look at a Greek myth from the 7th century BCE that is central to our Western culture and that portrays the struggle for power. Hesiod's *Theogony*[1] tells of the 'constitution' of the world amidst discord, struggle and betrayal, with the gods fighting for power. Hesiod describes the original state of the universe (Cosmos) as Chaos, the void from which everything sprang. Next came Gaia (Earth), Tartarus (Darkness) and Eros (Love). One of Gaia's children was Uranus (Sky), with whom Gaia mated to produce twelve children, the Titans, including Cronos (Time). Upon their birth, a struggle ensued that lasted for generations and involved cruelty between father and children and among brothers for control of the Cosmos. One of the children of Cronos, Zeus, ultimately triumphed and brought order to the universe. Hesiod's *Theogony* can clearly be seen as an early representation of human destiny as a competition for power wherein love plays a minor role.

The fascination with power and dominion has persisted throughout history. A classic work on the power struggle often used in management and political strategy is *The Prince*, by Niccolò

Machiavelli (1469-1527).[2] In this essay dedicated to a prince of the Medici family, Machiavelli advises on how to attain power and ensure survival. He maintains that he has no interest in an *imagined ideal,* but is concerned with *reality*, informed by reason,[3] and believes that contradictions have to be faced. In *The Prince,* he determines that the appropriate course of action is imposed by necessity and must recognize circumstances. While the aphorism 'The ends justify the means' is often ascribed to Machiavelli, commentators like Philip Bobbitt maintain that this is incorrect and that a more appropriate translation of "*si guarda al fine*" is: "One must consider the outcome".[4]

In his essay, Machiavelli describes the manipulative means a prince can use to attain power. The key concept he uses is *virtù,* usually conveyed as ability, talent, strength, power, skill or ingenuity.[5] It can be seen as the quality that serves ambition, by enabling a prince to withstand the blows of fortune, secure his government and rise to glory.[6] It is accompanied by prudence in risk-taking and calculated cunning.[7] The objective is to keep the prince in power. Despite the apparent endorsement of duplicity and deception in *The Prince* and its prevailing interpretation, there are diverse opinions as to what message Machiavelli actually intended.[8]

We should not simply deduce that he assumed human nature to be evil; rather, it seems, he believed that humans are affected by the historical context in which they live.[9] Although some say that Machiavelli defends moral decadence in *The Prince* as a means to attain and maintain power, in his other book, *Discourses on Livy,*[10] he writes that a republic presupposes a public-spirited man with a love of liberty. Drawing on the Roman republican ideal of the common good, he discusses how cities can come to greatness if the good of the community is placed above private interest.[11] Here he is influenced by the civic humanist movement of his time, itself inspired to seek the common good by Livy's idea[12] of the republican model.

Roman history, however, comprised two opposing realities: a virtuous republic defended by stalwart soldiers and guardians of public liberty; and a corrupt empire,[13] where citizens, obsessed with power and wealth, gave priority to their personal interests. In order to promote a common purpose, Machiavelli gives us the example of several admirable individuals and stresses the important role of law, as any foundation requires *ordini,* or institutions, if it is to endure. Machiavelli writes: "just as good customs require laws in order to be maintained, so laws require good customs in order to be observed".[14] From this, we can deduce that good laws induce good citizenship and civic behaviour reinforces the law. Good institutions can influence citizens to act for the common good. This is an optimistic view, for it shows that we are capable of shaping a better destiny through law, good governance and civic behaviour. Even if the human being may not be perfect, the outcome of civic action can be beneficial and is dependent on the legal framework of its time.

A century after Machiavelli's *The Prince,* another central work on political theory, Thomas Hobbes's *Leviathan*, was published. Hobbes (1588-1679) lived in England in the midst of great unrest that culminated in the Civil War, during the closing period of which he wrote his book. Leviathan is Hobbes's term for the state or *res publica.* It is a mythical *animale artificial* or artificial being, representing the state and variously described as man, animal and machine.[15] Hobbes suggests that the violent urge in humans can only be contained by the might of the state.[16] The leviathan "state" continuously holds down the behemoth (beast) or "revolutionary people". Thus, the terror that violence evokes in everyone results in a voluntary ceding of rights in return for protection – a social contract imposing peace through artificial chains, or civil laws.

The dark reality of the time in which he lived makes understandable Hobbes's pessimistic vision of human nature, involving persistent conflict, strife and fear for one's life. In his book he observes that human lives are "nasty, brutish and short", a monstrous condition, against which humans are condemned to struggle. Hobbes explains human existence in terms of appetites, desires and fear. Hope represents the possible satisfaction of appetite. And the greatest fear is that of violence and death. He suggests that society must be organized around fear, in order to protect property and life. In his vision, the road to peace is through the voluntary harnessing of appetites, an action motivated by fear. The resulting 'social contract', whereby all voluntarily relinquish their totally free movements to a sovereign state that governs via laws, preserves everyone from violence and ensures peace. Those who enter the covenant are elevated to a unified person, the state, with power of punishment and reward, in order to keep violent behaviour in check.

We can understand Hobbes better by looking at his other work, *De Cive* (*On the Citizen*), which was published in Latin in Paris in 1642, almost a decade before the *Leviathan.* In it, like Machiavelli in *Discourses,* he turns to the history of Rome, but focuses on the violence and decadence of the last days of the Roman Empire. Thus inspired and observing the history of his own times, he writes of the inconsistency between what humans say and how they act. Although proclaiming Justice and Charity ("Man to Man is a kind of God"), in order to protect themselves, they act by necessity with deceit and violence ("Man to Man is an arrant Wolfe").[17] The only way to resolve this contradiction is through law and contracts, the "rudiments both of morall and of civill prudence".[18] Morals cannot be trusted without restraint. Justice comes not from nature but from consent, from humans entering into a covenant.

Hobbes writes that by nature, humans have no moral constraints, but he is non-judgemental in his assessment. A famous line from De Cive describes "men as if they had just emerged from the earth like mushrooms and grown up without any obligation to each other".[19] Men enter society in the same way that mushrooms grow in the woods. As they feel no obligation to each other, Hobbes observes that in the realm of property, it is natural for people to contend for a greater share. However, people shun violence in any ensuing struggle that might lead to dissolution. Realizing that desires have to be constrained and in order to avoid anarchy, men are willing to enter into a contract that imposes restraint.

Hobbes's political theory is one that arises from practical observation of human history. His role is important as he lays the foundation for law as the basis for a peaceful civil society, even if he assumes that humans have no moral sense and so his goal is not the *summum bonum* or the greatest good, upheld by Machiavelli in *Discourses* and by John Locke[20] in *Two Treatises on Government.* Because Hobbes believes that it is around fear that society must be organized, he does not try to transform the social contract into a state of harmony, because state and revolution, leviathan and behemoth, are potentially always present. Fear persists.

This dark vision of human nature continued with Bernard Mandeville (1670-1733), in his poem, *The Fable of the Bees: or, Private Vices, Publick Benefits*. One of the most successful authors of the 18th century, Mandeville uses the allegory of a beehive to describe how dishonesty and selfishness, manifested in a desire for personal gain, actually lead to thriving. Dissatisfied at having their viciousness associated with prosperity, the bees complain about the poor state of their morals and ask the gods to intercede. With their wish fulfilled, the hive is made honest and virtuous, but without the motivation of greed, their activity subsides: "They flew into a hollow tree, blest with content and honesty".[21]

Mandeville believes that all things exist to satisfy selfish desires. Even altruistic motivation serves to gratify vanity. Thus, from the standpoint of his rigorist formula, all things are vicious. Since all is vicious, even things beneficial to us arise from vicious causes, and private vices are thus public benefits. For Mandeville, a benefit is anything that is useful, productive and leads to national prosperity and happiness.[22] Vice is thus the foundation of prosperity and happiness. While human desires and ambition are essentially evil, resulting in private vices, the acquisitive desire, manifest through spending and invention, creates prosperity and wealth and hence public benefit. Thrift on the other hand results in inactivity and public poverty.

Mandeville's work is often used as an endorsement of greed, which is seen as permitting progress. Virtue, by contrast, results in apathy and stagnation. His fable justifies acquisitive ambition and self-serving competition. No act is meritorious. Historians attribute Adam Smith's treatment of self-interest and division of labour and competition, resulting in the invisible hand, to Mandeville's influence. However, Smith might not have agreed. He refers to Mandeville's philosophy as a 'licentious system' and presents a careful discussion of it in *The Theory of Moral Sentiments,* where he contrasts self-love and aspiration for the best in human nature with selfishness and vanity: "one is a just, reasonable and equitable passion, while the other is unjust, absurd, and ridiculous". He also speaks of Mandeville's fallacy in seeing luxury and sensibility as vices. For Smith, the arts and aesthetics allow improvements in human life.[23]

Thus, we see humans represented in mythology and in treatises written over millennia as covetous, deceitful and manipulative, driven by fear, and most would say this is human nature. But, rather than being perceived as negative, these attributes are seen as contributing to the thriving of society, to success and progress, and any excess is constrained through the social contract or law. By the same token, a society lacking such covetous motivation is seen to stagnate. This vision of human egoism, competition and fear forms the backdrop to economic and financial management as they are generally practised, with Adam Smith's ideas of self-interest and the invisible hand serving as justification, even though this is a misrepresentation of Smith's view. Contrary to the prevailing interpretation of his thinking, Smith's self-interest entails virtue and sympathy.

Ideas, Language and Custom: The Person

Montaigne, in his essay 'On Habit', scandalized his contemporaries by claiming that "the laws of conscience, which we say are born of nature, are born of custom".[24] Whether we adhere to the idea of an innate conscience or not, most now acknowledge that custom influences behaviour. Our conventional perception of human nature is informed by a pessimistic view, which may be justified by our violent history, but encompasses just part of the human being. It is supposedly informed by reality and by scientific observation. But science offers a description, and not necessarily a full understanding. Moreover, scientific positions change, and the current view of human nature is that it is capable of empathy and collaboration and not necessarily purely egoistical.

Although many believe we are trapped in the reality of unending strife, are we condemned to this destiny? Our perception of human nature can change, and the person evolves. Contrary to Hobbes's pessimistic view, based on fear, can we shape social relations and our rapport with institutions and the state by evoking a more positive view of humanity and thus evolving social norms towards a kinder future? Does destiny control us or can we influence destiny? It is paradoxical that in our times, when we believe we can dominate the outer world with science and technology, we are incapable of dominating our inner world – our view of our own nature – and leading our social evolution along a more beneficial path. Our future is not immutable. History is not simply filled with stories of atrocities, of abuse and domination, but also with humane stories of kindness and cooperation. As Livy writes, history is full of "fine things to take as models, base things, rotten through and through, to avoid".[25]

In order to shape a better future, we must evolve ideas, change the language of custom and, in this way, we may hope to arrive at a transformation of behaviour and new possibilities. At the centre of any transformation is the person. How do we understand the person? As a solitary individual fighting for existence or an integral part of society building a common ground? Hopelessly lost in egoistical isolation or connected to the whole through empathy? How does one person relate to another? Through fear or trust? Through greed or sympathy? Through extortion or contribution? Does evil or good predominate? Is not the human being part of the intrinsic order of the universe? Do we not desire peace and happiness? Is not the common good a precondition for both?

With the predominance of science, we have forgotten the spirit, and as a result we have lost sight of a vital dimension of the person. In exploring the concept of the person, Jacques Maritain[26] points to the deficiency of our language and the limitation of our ideas. He questions: "Is not the *person* the self? Is not *my person my self?*" The self is not simply the ego. The human being has two poles: the material, which concerns the individual, and the spiritual, which concerns the person. The individual (ego) derives from matter and the person (generosity) from the spirit. Good is compromised when we give too much weight to the individual aspect of our being, expressed via egoism. The humanistic tradition espoused by Aristotle, and reinforced by Aquinas and others, includes within its essence the desire to serve the human being. It states that the common good is the *human* common good.

Maritain writes that society provides the person with the conditions for existence and personal development. It provides material goods but also the means to satisfy emotional and spiritual needs. Society nourishes, and is in turn fed by, the people who form the community. It is a dynamic social body, with each affecting the whole, and not just the sum of separate individuals. Each person is related to the entire community as the part to the whole, and the person does not reach plenitude alone. The common good of the city is not the mere collection of private goods. It is the good *human* life of the multitude of persons; it is their communion in good living. It is worth comparing this discussion with John Locke's view of civil society, and contrasting both with Thomas Hobbes's, where the common good is not considered.

The common good includes the collection of public commodities and services, but also something more profound and more human. It includes the sum of the civic conscience: liberty, political virtues and the sense of what is right. It comprises material prosperity and human wealth, including wisdom, morality, justice, friendship and happiness. All these aspects constitute the good human life of the people. The common good is not simply a system of advantages and utilities, but an end good in itself – *bonum honestum,* as expressed by the ancient philosophers. It ensures the just and morally good existence of the community. The life of a person is not a mere social or economic utility. The common good is ethically good and implies that people are fully engaged as committed citizens. The common good is not just that of a nation, but of the whole world, for nations make up the world. When we, by extension, connect ourselves to nature, we make possible the common good of the universe, including nature within which we live.

Recovering Virtue

To attain a destiny that respects the human being at the centre of society, we must re-establish a language of values that has been increasingly lost in recent times. 'Virtue' is a word still seldom used today, even though the discussion of ethics has increased in the wake of financial and other scandals. Companies have ethical codes and profess to adopt ethical principles, but in many cases they have proven to be empty words, used for promotional purposes. In modern culture, morality is seen as subjective and restrictive and we tend to avoid judging character as good or bad. Martin Luther King's dream half a century ago of his children being judged not by the colour of their skin but by the strength of their character[27] has been lost.

Rather than looking at *character*, development of the person in psychological and social circles has focused on the individual *personality*. The movement towards freedom of thought and action and globalization, opening up our awareness of a wealth of different cultures, has meant that an agreed idea of morality lost its sway.[28] Rather than being fixed guides, morals have come to be viewed as relative values, necessarily differing from culture to culture, as potentially curbing freedom and, with the exposure of hypocrisy, the moral ideal has lost ground and credibility. In a world increasingly focused on concrete material progress, a system of principles guided by moral standards has ceased to be considered fundamental to the human being. People have become defined by what they possess and not by who they are. Material achievement has gained precedence over human flowering; nothing could impede material advance.

However, in classical Greece, the material did not over-ride virtue, a central value that ensures the wellbeing of the *polis,* the city state. Aristotle writes that harmony in the *polis* is only possible through virtue.[29] It is a "habit, accompanied with deliberate preference, in the relative mean, defined by reason". It is a mean[30] or balanced state between two states of vice, one representing excess and the other deficit. A man's chief good is the "activity of the soul according to virtue... for as neither one swallow, nor one day, makes a spring; so neither does one day, nor a short time, make a man blessed and happy". For Aristotle, happiness is not a passing state, but a life well lived. It is only possible through a life of virtue, which permits *eudaimonia* or flourishing,[31] seen as *telos* or the ultimate purpose of life. Virtue commands and illuminates a life and affords it happiness. Whereas morality implies a system of principles or rules imposed from without, virtue is a state of being that flows from within the person through good purposeful action.

The economist Robert Skidelsky and Edward, his philosopher son, aim to revive economics as a moral science and make a distinction between needs and wants in their book, *How Much Is Enough?* They see economics as a science of human beings in communities, not of interacting robots. They describe the pursuit of endless growth as senseless. Rather, growth should be seen as a means to obtain basic goods and the good things in life, which the Skidelskys list as health, security, respect, friendship, leisure, harmony with nature, and personality, or autonomy, which according to Kant is the capacity to express oneself. These are goods that are universal, indispensable and *sui generis,* i.e., they are not means to other goods, but ends in themselves. The Skidelskys write that restoration of leisure, as opposed to idleness or passive consumption, will help put the desire for monetary gain into proper perspective as well as encouraging a recognition of the difference between *needs* and *wants,* between the essential and the dispensable. They recognize that their proposed agenda would mean a redefinition of many of the presuppositions in economics, but they see the adoption of such an agenda as vital, or "we are a doomed civilization".[32]

The Skidelskys remind us of Keynes's view that people have finite material needs which might one day be fully satisfied. In his essay, 'Economic Possibilities for our Grandchildren', Keynes writes that with the satisfaction of material needs, humans can "take wings into the future".[33] A world of economic prosperity would entail the end of toil, but also a readjustment in how we live: "To those who sweat for their daily bread leisure is a longed-for sweet until they get it... for we have been trained too long to strive and not to enjoy". If we do take wings, the love of money as a possession will be recognized as a "somewhat disgusting morbidity". In such a world, the blind pursuit of wealth will no longer be applauded or encouraged. Rather the human being will aim to secure "immortality for his acts by pushing his interest in them forward into time". In other words, this would entail caring for future generations. To achieve Keynes's vision, we require a yearning for more than the material. It involves a regard for human dignity, empathy and responsibility.

Social psychologists today view a virtuous life as too demanding and impossible to achieve for it entails consistency in behaviour, a unified person. People are seen to respond according to the context: one who is honest in one situation can be dishonest in another. This in fact represents fragmentation of the person. Many sociologists believe that, because virtue is an ideal that humans fall so far short of attaining, it is not reasonable to consider it in practice. It is an abstract ideal that is unattainable. We make up values as projections of our preferences. As in economics, preferences rule. Modern philosophers and economists measure the strength of beliefs by 'assigning subjective probabilities' and of preferences by assigning 'utilities'. It is a mathematical game, even in the subjective world.

Like economists, philosophers propounding 'rational choice theory'[34] think we should pick options on the basis of expected costs and benefits.[35] Action is guided by such calculation, and the rational choice is seen as that which promotes self-interest, represented by units of material welfare. However, the philosopher Hilary Putnam writes that "real ethical questions... involve a complex mixture of philosophical beliefs, religious beliefs, and factual beliefs as well"[36] and criticizes this objective approach to ethics. Reducing the treatment of ethical issues – so vital to our existence – to measurement, and lowering a human ideal to the level of our limitations is to deprive humanity of its ontological meaning, of its ultimate dream, its transcendent possibilities and its richness. It is to impoverish humanity.

It is true that virtue is difficult to achieve. Martha Nussbaum writes that many of the constituents of a life well lived through virtue, permitting *eudaimonia,* are outside the control of most.[37] Aristotle himself notes that success in attaining this is in part dependent on external goods: friends, wealth, political power and above all the advantage of good birth, satisfactory children and personal beauty.[38] This may appear elitist in our world. However, Aristotle is actually discussing the role that fate can play in facilitating our flourishing through good actions and how catastrophe may impede us. It is true, for example, that good birth and wealth may assist us through our social position to achieve political effect. But we need virtue to guide us in the definition of political action that benefits the whole. In particular, Aristotle believes that *philia* or friendship facilitates virtue.

He also writes that good fortune is "something different from happiness".[39] He writes that "to conclude that the cause of happiness was external goods... would be as if anyone should suppose that the playing well upon the lyre was owing to the instrument, and not to the art".[40] Thus, we should not resign ourselves to fate. While material goods may depend on fortune, it is not fortune alone that makes someone wise and just. And among the goods enumerated above, friendship and interior beauty can be cultivated and children are formed by education. How we use external goods determines whether the outcome will be happy. Both Aristotle and Aquinas opine on the importance of virtue for the common good, which comprises material goods and the human good, as we saw in our earlier discussion of Jacques Maritain.

Alasdair MacIntyre discusses Aristotle's view that the practice of virtue requires good action. Deliberation on virtue is insufficient. Virtue requires more than intellectual qualities; it demands a "particular kind of initiation and participation in a particular kind of moral and political practice".[41] There is no blueprint, no philosophical or theoretical statement that can determine the exact course of action, but it requires considered action in dialogue and shared purpose. MacIntyre suggests embodying the precepts of natural law in the conception of a social and political order. As with Aristotle, he believes virtue is achieved through a life well lived in civic action. What would it take to achieve this goal?

The Dalai Lama writes that the ethical void is so deep in today's world that it must be remedied not only through religious channels, the normal avenues for ethical teaching, but through secular channels as well.[42] He points to the social, economic and environmental difficulties that exist in the world. He attributes them, despite technological and economic advances, to a major lack of moral ethics and inner values. Ethics involve personal responsibility and inner values stem from compassion. He writes: "Ultimately, any system, any set of laws or procedures, can only be as effective as the individuals responsible for its implementation. If, owing to failures of personal integrity, a good system is misused, it can easily be a source of harm rather than a source of benefit."

Referring to business and finance, the Dalai Lama says that "the systems themselves may be sound, but if the people using them are unscrupulous and driven by self-serving greed, the benefits of those systems will be undermined... Ultimately, the source of our problem lies at the level of the individual. If people lack moral values and integrity, no system of laws and regulations will be adequate. So long as people give priority to material values, then injustice, corruption, inequity, intolerance, and greed – all the outward manifestations of neglect of inner values – will persist." Hence, the need for inner values in our age of science and technology is more pressing than ever and requires the participation of everyone, both religious and secular. Inner values are stronger than any division.

The Dalai Lama believes that if we see human nature as grounded on destructive tendencies, then we must ground any restraint on something outside of ourselves. We would need law to restrain us. But if we view human nature as predominantly oriented towards a desire for good and for peace, then we allow ourselves the innate potential to realize a life that is naturally and rationally ethical. Self-regulation then can complement external rules. Human potential plays a major role in realizing the kind of world we would like to see. For the Dalai Lama, such a vision would require only the recognition of two principles: 1) our shared humanity and shared aspiration to happiness and the avoidance of suffering; and 2) understanding interdependence as a key feature of human reality. This is based not on idealism, but a *true understanding of reality*, that of our shared humanity and our interdependence.

Restoring Justice

In contemporary political philosophy, John Rawls's account of 'justice as fairness' makes the value of fairness, or a lack of bias and of vested interests, central to political morality. It informs the establishment of principles, the setting up of just institutions and the passing of legislation to ensure that principles are upheld.[43] The first principle of justice is liberty and the second is distribution, which implies that the worst-off members of society must be as well off as possible. This involves the distribution of primary goods, which include "rights, liberties and opportunities, income and wealth, and the social bases of self-respect", achieved through the operation of incentives.

Rawls points to the moral powers that people have and their capacity for a conception of the good, rather than simply a sense of self-interest and prudence. He emphasizes perfect institutions and law but assumes that the human propensity for good is present to ensure that institutions and law are respected: "if other persons with evident intention strive to do their part in just or fair arrangements, citizens tend to develop trust and confidence in them".[44] The economist John Kenneth Galbraith argues for "countervailing power" in order to avoid corruption of power, and points to the American ideal of a multiplicity of institutions that check and balance the force and domination of any one institution.[45] The legal framework enables ethical action. Hence, the virtue of justice practised by the individual is fortified by just institutions; they complement each other.[46] Justice cannot co-exist with corrupt institutions.

Rather than theorizing about justice, Amartya Sen is concerned with enhancing justice and removing injustice. While he recognizes the importance of institutions, he believes justice is ultimately connected with people's lives and linked to human *capability*, which is partly dependent on opportunity and freedom of action to influence outcome. To illustrate this, he refers to early Indian jurisprudence from Sanskrit literature: *niti,* relating to organizational propriety and behavioural correctness, and *nyaya,* the realization of justice. Sen posits that "a question that awaits examination is whether advantage-seeking... provides the only robust basis of reasonable behaviour in society. A related question is whether mutual benefit and reciprocity must be the foundation of all political reasonableness."[47] This is the foundation for the common good. Sen advocates "government by discussion"[48] as a quality of democracy. This involves not simply electing representatives and handing to them our destiny, but participating in the way that society evolves through discussion and action. This is how we can influence the world in which we live and shape it well.

One of the most popular political philosophers today, Michael Sandel, points to three concepts of justice as espoused by Aristotle (virtue and the good life), Rawls (freedom) and Sen (maximizing welfare). He questions whether a just society should encourage the virtue of its citizens.[49] While in ancient philosophical thinking, such as Aristotle's, justice starts with virtue, modern thinking such as Rawls's places the emphasis on freedom. Because in democratic societies there is disagreement about preferences and beliefs and because we value freedom, we are loath to pronounce on the right course of action.

In *On Liberty*, John Stuart Mill writes that people should be free to do whatever they want, provided they do no harm to others. But Mill also subscribes to the idea that the highest end of human life is the full and free development of the human faculties, i.e., the formation of character. He distinguishes between the higher and the lower pleasures and believes that the ideal of human dignity, independent of our wants and desires, sets the standard.

Sandel proposes that as a society we should agree on what the common good is, for then virtue and freedom are aligned. He writes that we can move from principles to moral argument only via reflection. What kind of world do we want? A purely material world? Or is it time to encourage humanistic ideals and not just material practicality? This is a reflection for today; it is not a solitary pursuit but a joint public endeavour,[50] a vital one.

In his vision for society, Pope Francis places the emphasis on human dignity. In his *Apostolic Exhortation: Evangelii Gaudium,* the Pope denounces a world where "everything comes under the laws of competition and the survival of the fittest, where the powerful feed upon the powerless... and where human beings are themselves considered consumer goods to be used and then discarded". He warns that we are moving beyond exploitation and oppression to a throw-away culture, a society where people are even treated as disposable. Pope Francis attributes the current financial crisis to a profound human crisis: the denial of the primacy of the person, giving way to a "dictatorship of an impersonal economy lacking a truly human purpose", where the human being is reduced to the sole purpose of consumption. He calls for the return of a code of ethics that "condemns the manipulation and debasement of the person" to "bring about balance and a more humane social order", where money serves and does not rule. He warns that "injustice tends to expand its baneful influence and quietly to undermine any political and social system, no matter how solid it may appear", leading to the risk of its disintegration. Yet he appeals to confidence against defeatism through faith in human potential.[51]

In his book *The Price of Inequality*, Joseph Stiglitz calls 'opportunity', the promise of equality, fairness and justice, a myth in America. He exposes the tacit agreement between the top echelons and the rest of society, whereby the top provides jobs and prosperity in exchange for bonuses and a share of profits. The subprime crisis shows this agreement to be front loaded and in fact exploitative of the poor and the less educated. Fault lines were created within the financial system and these eventually cracked.[52] Stiglitz attributes the lack of accountability, in the face of financial collapse, to a major problem in our economic and political systems, exposing imperfect institutions, contrary to Rawls's vision discussed above. In the aftermath of the financial crisis, it became clear that the political system has not served society: it failed to prevent the crisis, to check the growing inequality, to protect those at the bottom and to prevent corporate abuse, all through lack of adequate supervision or appropriate policy.

This awareness led to mass demonstrations in Spain with the *indignados* and then in New York with the Occupy movement, which subsequently spread to London and other cities. Citizen awareness and public consciousness were raised and the public discourse altered. The public became aware that government had aligned itself with special moneyed interests and that supervisory organizations lacked the power to apportion responsibility and correct the problem. Government policy is gradually changing with recognition of the extent of public discontent. Financial legislation is being passed and prosecution of banks for contravening the law has gained pace. Caps on banking bonuses have been set in Europe and compensation reform is beginning in the UK. However, the work is far from done. As long as financial agents seek to defeat[53] or bypass legislation and to find loopholes, justice cannot be done nor trust recovered. In discussing the creation of institutions to ensure justice, Rawls points to the importance of confidence in institutional guarantees of the good of society. Instead we have seen wrongdoing and violation of the common good and the use of loopholes to avoid legal compliance. Moral direction has been lost, exposing the corruption of society. The moral compass has to be realigned through virtue, without which justice cannot be realized, even with reinforced regulation.

We have seen that, for Aristotle, justice is a central virtue that enables all virtues, and it governs proportionality in exchange. For proportionality or justice in the distribution of wealth, temperance is required. Greed prompts excessive extraction and greed is the opposite of temperance. In the 18th century, the 3rd Earl of Shaftesbury, who refutes any egoistic vision, writes: "If the regard toward [acquisition of wealth] be moderate... there is nothing in this case which is not compatible with virtue, and even suitable and beneficial to society. But if it grows at length into a real passion; the injury and mischief it does the public, is not greater than that which it creates to the person himself."[54] He examines the human being first as an individual unit and secondly in his or her wider relations to the larger units of society and the universe of humankind. As with Aristotle, we note the principle of harmony or balance, with the impulse for satisfaction of one's appetites in accord with the impulse for the realization of the good of society. Hence, the satisfaction of one's desires can neither clash with nor jeopardize the common good.

Virtue and Dignity in Markets

Classic economic theory states that market exchange is made possible because the transaction provides benefits to everyone who is party to it (Adam Smith's 'invisible hand'). It assumes voluntary action and individuals motivated by self-interest. The market works by engaging with each individual's private interest. Any regard for another's interest is seen to require sacrifice. Market theory discards the idea of mutual benefit as a goal, but assumes it as a given outcome. It is built into trade via the willingness to pay, thereby determining the price level at which transactions occur. Markets are mere contracts without any moral content. Virtue is perceived as unnecessary for markets to achieve their purpose.

However, we have not seen financial markets functioning perfectly, as economic market theory would make us believe. Unfettered markets left unchecked for the purpose of maximizing gain can feed avarice, encourage fraud and result not in mutual benefit but gross inequality in distribution and often losses to the victims of manipulative or fraudulent activity. Such market agents pay no heed to justice, the ultimate virtue, nor to human dignity.

Adam Smith, even if he does not think benevolence necessary for transactions in society, believes justice to be indispensable: "the prevalence of injustice must utterly destroy it".[55] Smith's economic synthesis was inspired by indignation over the suffering and humiliation inflicted by feudal masters and the monopolization of benefits through mercantilism. He believed the market could be humanizing and provide dignity, with beggars relieved from begging via paid work. In his view, the market is a 'tool' of genuine sociality, even if not a place of friendship.[56]

Luigino Bruni and Robert Sugden describe a market where virtue can prevail, while maintaining the instrumentality of markets,[57] and use as an illustration the thinking of Antonio Genovesi (1713-1769), the Neapolitan economist, for whom the two foundations of civil society are justice and humanity. Writing in the same period as Adam Smith, Genovesi believes in the human inclination towards mutual assistance and sees 'reciprocity' as a fundamental feature of human nature. For him, reciprocity is the bond of society; it is mutually reinforcing. Reciprocal confidence, public trust, mutual assistance and friendship or fraternity are essential preconditions for civil and commercial society. Fraternity implies goodwill and mutual respect. Genovesi's concept of 'confidence' has a strongly moral content: each has to be confident of the probity, justice and virtue of others. Bruni and Sugden argue that market transactions depend on trust and work best when parties do not breach confidence. Contrary to what prevailing market theory leads us to believe, market interactions need not be merely instrumental and impersonal, operating in a 'morally free zone', separate from social or communal relationships. They can be fraternal, without any implication of self-sacrifice.[58]

In order for a commercial society to function well, there has to be confidence in everyone's intention to honour contracts and to eschew fraud, and in the effectiveness and integrity of the legal system. Thus, if a nation is to develop economically, a first priority for government is to cultivate public trust. The legal framework sets the conditions, but this is not possible without every agent respecting the law and contributing to the realization of its principles. A breakdown in trust leads to market failure as we have seen with the great financial crisis unleashed in 2008. No market or society can be separately self-interested, without regard for the common good, for long. The inherent faults in such a system, with abuse of power or exploitation by greed, will eventually be exposed and, in order to be corrected, mutual benefit must perforce be reintroduced.

In our current context, the prevailing understanding of markets is that anything is for sale at a price. Michael Sandel criticizes the extension of market principles into spheres of life where they do not belong.[59] In our world market economics can govern the most personal of human relations, including marriage. He sees our moral dilemma as partly due to this fact and not only to greed, which is a reason often cited. Sandel calls for a public debate about the role of markets and their moral limits. His reasons are twofold: inequality and corruption. Are markets indeed free? The presence of inequality can undermine meaningful consent. A world where everything is for sale is even less humane for those of limited means and putting a price on a relational transaction corrupts it by tainting and degrading it.

We have to call into question the extensive use of monetary incentives, which determine the course of modern life. They are seen to optimize economic efficiency, thus maximizing social utility, which is understood in economics as the sum of people's preferences, measured in monetary terms. An efficient allocation of resources is believed to maximize the economic wellbeing of all members of society. However, contrary to this theory, the wellbeing of all has not been served in our market economy. Sandel argues that monetary incentives should not be used to solve all social problems. There are goods that should not have a monetary price, because relational transactions are not merely market mechanisms; they embody values worth caring about. The pre-eminence of money results in the lowering of norms and the removal of the stigma relating to transgressive behaviour. Certain behaviour *should* be discouraged, even stigmatized.

Sandel writes that the lack of moral content in contemporary politics stems in part from this corruption; money reigns supreme and there is no discussion of the good life in the Aristotelian sense of a life well lived. Citizens are asked to leave their moral and spiritual convictions behind when they enter the public square.[60] Our social norms accept that human behaviour in public life need not be governed by moral principles. Sandel's argument helps us understand that the moral and political challenges we face today go beyond finance to the role and reach of markets in our social practices, human relationships and everyday lives. From this we can conclude that, as long as maximization of money is accepted as the primary motivation, our tolerance of destructive behaviour is increased. Morality is seen to be an ideal, whereas money represents reality, and reality takes precedence over the ideal. Thus, in recent decades we have remade social relations into market relations. Money has vanquished virtue.

The Common Good

The common good underlies humanism and a civil economy that serves the human being. Ernesto Screpanti and Stefano Zamagni (a proponent of Genovesi's 'civil economy') write that the humanist is an "active subject, open to innovation, a lover of freedom who is proud of his civil virtues... [combining] action and reflection, art and accountancy, religion and politics, theory and practice to create a world with space for his own freedom".[61] Humanism implies a unifying process that encompasses all aspects of life and involves a cultural dimension, including the arts, literature, philosophy and law. Inspired by the Roman ideal of a good republic, freedom is an essential condition. We can ask what freedom entails. It is not found in acting exactly as we wish without restraint.

The philosopher, Jean-Paul Sartre, discusses the interconnection between liberty and responsibility in his lecture, *Existentialism is a Humanism,*[62] and notes that our freedom depends on the other's freedom and the other's on our own. Liberty is founded on commitment, in a 'will to freedom', and this entails responsibility to ensure the other's freedom, as soon as we *will* our own. It is like a mirror image. There is no true freedom for oneself without the same for fellow humans. Another philosopher known for his work on ethics, Paul Ricoeur, also believes that each person's liberty is fully dependent on that of the other, i.e. that one person's liberty cannot be at the expense of another's. Ricoeur states: "The moral law commands us to make the highest possible good in the world the final object of all our conduct".[63] He advances as an ethical foundation a regard for the other as oneself.

As important as freedom to humanism is the belief that interpersonal relationships are the true economic resource, as discussed above in the section on Genovesi. This goes beyond money into reciprocity and friendship. Humanism is civil and it entails the common good. Thus, the common good presupposes humanistic principles and involves personal choice. It concerns the 'total person' and not just the material. It implies mutual benefit and not advantage-seeking. The common good is not just a system of advantages and utilities, but something deeper. Each person, governed by virtuous behaviour within a *polis* or state, contributes to the total wellbeing of the group. The governance framework inspires trust and confidence for it is based on justice and respect. Humanism implies a life well lived and as such permits *eudaimonia,* or human flourishing. This is a precondition of happiness. To most this may appear beyond our human capacity, but there is always a starting point. What is our vision for the person and for our world? We are free to choose how we act, and the sum of individual actions shapes the world. Acting virtuously makes for a better world, and virtue is facilitated by compassion and love.

Chapter 5

Compassion and Collaboration: Understanding True Self-Interest

"Three passions, simple but overwhelmingly strong have governed my life: the longing for love, the search for knowledge, and unbearable pity for the suffering of mankind."
Bertrand Russell

"Our human compassion binds us the one to the other – not in pity or patronizingly, but as human beings who have learnt how to turn our common suffering into hope for the future."
Nelson Mandela

"Anyone appearing to be wanting in compassion is called inhuman, and so 'humanity' is often used as its synonym."
Arthur Schopenhauer

Language, Perception and Culture
Shifting Landscape?
Compassion and Understanding
Compassion Permitting Virtue
Collaboration through Empathy
Understanding True Self-Interest

~~~

We have seen how human motivation influences society in general, including economic and financial outcomes. Good outcomes are not possible without virtue or ethical behaviour. A pessimistic view of the person as driven by egoism and ruled by fear does not favour beneficial outcomes. Instead, if the person is seen as motivated by compassion and as having a regard for the other, the result is the practice of virtue and collaboration towards a good society. Such a regard implies *true self-interest* in a complex and interconnected world. A positive view of the human being is increasingly adopted, including in the field of science.

~~~

Language, Perception and Culture

Virtue is facilitated by compassion as compassion leads to altruism, or action in regard for the other. In *The Social Conquest of Earth*, Edward O. Wilson, the biologist and naturalist, makes his case for evolution leading towards altruism. Noting the *eusociability* (literally 'true social condition') of insect colonies, such as ants and bees, where the insects work and care for each other across generations and beyond immediate kinship, he writes that human beings are further evolved. We are unique in possessing high intelligence, language and culture. Through language we are able, from infancy, to read other people's intentions. This has allowed for evolution of the mind, development of cultural traits and the evolution of morals.

The human being is made up not just of genetic material but also of a brain, sensory system and behaviour that develop after birth. In fact, Wilson writes that cultural evolution tends to overwhelm genetic evolution. Wilson describes morals as helping natural selection by passing along behaviour that best promotes the survival of one's species. Group dynamics through group selection, not selfish genes, form instincts that promote altruism.[1] This is a biological explanation of how language helps to shape perception, culture and behaviour.

In *Language, Consciousness, Culture*, Ray Jackendoff, a leading linguist and philosopher, offers another useful viewpoint. He explains the role of attention and language in understanding our civilizational challenge. Jackendoff poses the following questions regarding "the intimate relationship among the development of language, the development of genuinely human thought, and the development of civilization... What sorts of concepts are necessary in order to achieve civilization? ...Exactly how does... awareness and attention... help support richer inference?" He goes on to say that "culture involves symbolic meaning... language is the symbolic expression of thought".

We are conscious human beings, and our attention permits awareness and understanding. Perception is a crucial feature of awareness, the functioning of attention, and it influences our understanding. Jackendoff writes that language facilitates intense attention, thereby giving expression to thought and perception and influencing culture. Without language there are no ideas, and without ideas there is no civilization, which results from actions that we have chosen. Reading Jackendoff leads me to wonder how our prevailing language shapes our society. Our language focuses on egoism, competition and profit maximization, helping in turn to shape the kind of society that we are part of. If we stress compassion, collaboration and sharing, can a different form of society emerge over time?

Jackendoff writes that "an important domain of human nature is social cognition, the ability to understand and engage in social interactions within culture and social institutions", informed by a collection of established principles. In this context, the basic entities of the 'social domain' or 'persons' operate. The predominant language used, as well as the words to which importance is attributed and our perception of these words, gives meaning to action. It determines how behaviour is viewed and what is tolerated, encouraged or stigmatized. Thus, how we express ourselves is an important roadmap for behaviour. Among the specialized capacities for social cognition, Jackendoff includes altruism, cooperation (joint intentions) and morality (rules and other normative principles) – all matters of interest to us.[2]

Shifting Landscape?

Our cultural perspective is shifting and in recent times the change has been gathering momentum. We have observed this with the Occupy movement and a new tone in political and economic language. Although derided for not proposing concrete action and policy, the Occupy movement has contributed to a change in public discourse and has perhaps influenced government policy. It is worth noting that the debate around Occupy Saint Paul in London led Rowan Williams, then Archbishop of Canterbury, to write an editorial in the *Financial Times* denouncing excessive executive compensation.[3] The following day, David Cameron criticized such practice, the first time he had spoken publicly about the issue.[4] Governments have since passed new rules on capping bonuses, as in the European Union,[5] and prohibiting golden hand-shakes and parachutes[6] and bonuses linked to certain transactions not seen to enhance corporate value, as in Switzerland.[7]

Some maintain that we have not seen real change in the economic and financial paradigm and if we examine financial market activity and media reporting around it, this criticism appears justified. Banks find ways around bonus caps, using the argument that such bonuses are indispensable for maintaining competitiveness.[8] The financial machine continues to give priority to short-term trading and quarterly profits and share buybacks and mergers and acquisitions, rather than any far-sighted investment programme that would respond to our economic, environmental and social challenges, and create jobs and enhance long-term welfare. But change takes time and is often hidden from view until transformation has occurred. Our consumption machine actually took a century to reach its apex. Thorstein Veblen was writing about conspicuous consumption in 1899,[9] but it was only after World War II that America led the move towards mass consumption, which accelerated with the debt economy encouraged in the Reagan era (1980s) and which then spread across the world.

Looking at consumer behaviour today, although the machine seems to be in overdrive, particularly in China and other newly rich countries, one can perceive a certain fatigue, in Europe and the United Kingdom, with conspicuous consumption. This may be partly due to the financial crisis leaving people with less disposable income, but the trend started even before that. What motivates many consumers today has changed since the consumption boom began in the 1980s. One cause is the increasing perception that having more material goods does not necessarily contribute to happiness. Another is an enhanced awareness of the impact of excessive consumption (and the resulting waste) on nature. Although we are a long way from a real shift towards responsible behaviour, we may have begun on the slow path to change. Its necessity has entered our consciousness, the first step to requisite action.

Compassion and Understanding

Myths give meaning to our lives and actions. Hesiod's tale of the 'constitution' of the world is one of competition and strife. Less well known is another story by Pherecydes of Syros, a pre-Socratic philosopher, who lived about a century after Hesiod, in the 6th century BCE. In this myth, he describes three primary deities existing in eternity: Zas (Zeus), Cronos (Time) and Chthonie (the depths of the earth). In order to wed Chthonie, Zeus descends from the heavens and takes the form of Eros (Love). Elaborate preparations for the wedding feast take place and Zeus weaves a magnificent robe on which he embroiders the earth, the sea and the abodes of the sea: mythical images of Ge (Earth) and Ogenos (Oceans). Placing the robe on Chthonie, he marries her. Through the investiture she is transformed into Ge,[10] marking the newly created earth as Ge's official sphere of influence. Zeus originates the world order, not by overpowering and ousting Cronos, but by uniting with the earth-goddess, Ge, in Cronos (Time). Thus, heaven and earth are made one for all time. This marriage, representing the creation of the world, is a Greek archetype for the *telos* or purpose of human life, with Zeus as the protector of the moral, social and political order, achieved through love and not strife. Through marriage and union Zeus brings about peace and harmony and sows unity in the universe (*unitas ordinis*).[11]

Pherecydes is said to have been the first to write about the nature of the gods, although Hesiod wrote about the gods and Thales about nature.[12] For this reason, Pherecydes of Syros is often referred to as one of the first philosophers. His vision is one which goes beyond the temporal need for power to a more profound human need, that of unity and harmony. His is perhaps a tale more inspiring for our times, where the conflict among humans and between humans and nature threatens our future. We are in great need of a vision that promotes unity.[13] By adopting this vision, we call upon a different destiny for ourselves. Of course, determining a destiny is not as simple as adopting a vision. It depends on action, but action is influenced by vision. So, what is the starting point of our vision for action? Are we egoists or humanists? To be a humanist is to incorporate regard for the other in our action. It is a vision of fraternity and not strife. It is a vision of unity and harmony, leading to happiness.

Although Pherecydes writes of love (Eros), we can use compassion as a starting point for such a vision. The etymology of the Latin word for compassion is 'co-suffering'. The 'passion' in 'compassion' derives from the Latin *pati*, to suffer. Martha Nussbaum, the philosopher, has written extensively about the role of compassion in political philosophy. She distinguishes between empathy and compassion[14] and describes empathy as involving twofold attention: imagining what it is like to be in the sufferer's position and yet remaining securely aware that one is not in that position. While she maintains that empathy is psychologically important as a guide to action, it does not suffice for compassion, which entails emotional involvement in the other.

Compassion involves understanding the feelings and suffering of others, accompanied by a desire to alleviate pain. It is not simply pity. It links us to others, disintegrates our separateness and gives us common purpose. It permits full sharing. The Dalai Lama discusses compassion as awareness of our 'shared humanity'.[15] To the extent that we understand our interlinked condition, collaboration and sharing become easier. There is an emotional aspect to compassion, but it is also cultivated, worked towards. It is not simply a passing, inconsequential feeling. It requires awareness and involves choice. This is the springboard for altruism, the antithesis of selfishness and a cornerstone of humanism. The Golden Rule, "Do unto others as you would have them do unto you", embodies compassion.[16]

In the past, compassion was often associated with Buddhism and with religion, although it has also preoccupied philosophers and sociologists. The 19th century philosopher Auguste Comte, known as the father of sociology, highlights the general properties of human nature which enable human existence.[17] He believes that humans have a spontaneous propensity towards furthering the wellbeing of society and seek it instinctively for its own sake, and not just for personal advantage; that we have a certain, although moderate, amount of natural benevolence. He coined the word 'altruism', deriving it from the French word *autrui,* which means 'other people'. Comte believes that individuals have a moral interest in renouncing egoism and in considering others. He arrives at the conclusion that love[18] is the true source of human happiness. He was inspired by the exemplary altruistic behaviour – motivated by love – of Clotilde de Vaux. She died about a year after they met, but her memory continued to influence his thinking. Comte believes in service to humanity and sees this as possible through de Vaux's example.

Believing that the good of humanity is the ultimate standard of right and wrong and that moral discipline consists in the cultivation of the general good, Comte infers that the good of others should be the only inducement to act. He believes no self-interest rivals the inherent human tendency to universal love. Hence, the golden rule of morality is to live for others, irrespective of religion. For him, this is the 'religion of humanity'. The thinking of Comte influenced important figures, such as John Stuart Mill, John Ruskin and Rabindranath Tagore.

However, Comte's views did not gain a firm footing due to his absolutist approach. His philosophy of positivism developed eventually into a system that was too rigid. Not leaving room for self-expression, he was seen to be authoritarian and even dictatorial. Mill eventually turned against Comte, criticizing him for transfiguring himself into the High Priest of the Religion of Humanity, and for systematizing positivism into a secular religion. Comte, however, cannot be overlooked because of his faith in altruism, a regard for the other, which was overshadowed in the 20th century by Sigmund Freud's theory of the ego, or egoism.[19]

In recent times, compassion has become an area of study within neuroscience.[20] This is starting to change the general perception of human nature, which is no longer necessarily seen as inherently egoistical but as having a capacity for altruism, stemming from compassion. In neuroscience, compassion is often referred to as empathy;[21] there is no distinction such as that highlighted by Nussbaum. It is defined as: 1) the cognitive awareness of another's internal states, i.e. thoughts, feelings, perceptions and intentions; and 2) the vicarious affective response to another person.[22] The late Francisco Varela, a renowned neuroscientist, Buddhist and friend of the Dalai Lama, advocated compassion. In his book, *Ethical Know-How: Action, Wisdom and Cognition*, he writes about the paradigm shift in cognitive sciences, of the emerging view that the proper units of knowledge are primarily *concrete;* they are embodied, because they have been lived.[23] Knowledge derives from specific experiences within space and time. Thus, cognition is understood as *enaction*. Varela explains that reality is dependent on the perceiver and inseparable from the structure of the perceiver. Although most of mental and active life is devoted to coping with the immediate and is informed by habit, important knowledge stems from reflection and conscious appreciation. In line with Pieper's discussion of the Scholastic understanding of knowledge, Varela writes of the importance of reflection, and other neuroscientists reinforce that view.

In Buddhist practice, compassion comes from the emptying of the self (*sunya*), thus opening the self up to universal understanding, or awareness. Varela writes that this point is crucial, as it is the golden thread that unites our self-understanding with an external and scientific account of mental functioning, for cognitive science denies the existence of a solid, centralized, unitary self (Freud's ego). Rather it is a virtual self with "micro-identities" that "arise and subside in a succession of shifting patterns", as a result of distinct experiences in "micro-worlds". Varela describes compassion not as sympathy but as transference, seen in psychoanalysis as the only true love possible, as the desire to make whole and substantial the fragments of our being. We can thus see compassion as the way in which we are united with the whole, where our separateness finds a home. This understanding of unification is similar to that of love.

Compassion, which comes with awareness, naturally leads to a sense of warmth and inclusiveness and interest in others.

In the Mahayana Buddhist tradition that Varela practised, emptiness or *sunyata* is accompanied by another equally central and complementary concern – 'compassion' or *karuna*.[24] Varela quotes a Buddhist teacher as follows: "When the reasoning mind no longer clings and grasps... one awakens into the wisdom with which one was born, and compassionate energy arises without pretence". Thus, wisdom or *bodhicitta* is the 'enlightened mind' or 'awakened heart'. In this way, compassion and love are intertwined. An important step towards wisdom consists in developing compassion for oneself.[25] Only then can our concern for those around us expand and can we begin to envision a more open-ended and non-egocentric awareness. Compassion follows no rules. Its highest aspiration is to be responsive to the needs of the particular situation. Thus, it is inseparable from wisdom. Unless rules are informed by wisdom, they become sterile – hindrances to compassionate action rather than conduits for its manifestation. If we seek solely self-improvement, we will reinforce the ego.[26] For Varela, the motivation cannot simply be the self, but the reflection of the other as an expression of the self, similar to the approach of Paul Ricoeur.[27]

Compassion Permitting Virtue

Just as the Dalai Lama sees compassion as a response to our ethical void, the philosopher Arthur Schopenhauer developed in the 19th century a moral theory based on the idea that compassion drives moral actions. Schopenhauer rejects ethics based solely on moral obligation and law; his is an ethics of being, virtue ethics, in which compassion is the source of the virtues of justice and loving kindness, the cardinal virtues from which all other virtues are derived.[28] In these terms, compassion permits virtue. Schopenhauer grounds his ethics in a comprehensive metaphysics, stressing the interconnectedness of all things and including nonhumans within the moral sphere. All actions ultimately have an impact on others. Moral characters apprehend themselves in the other and pursue the other's wellbeing as if it were their own. The will is important, for action involves choice. Schopenhauer writes that all satisfaction and wellbeing and happiness consist of this "great mystery of ethics", for "as soon as this compassion is aroused... the difference between him and me is now no longer absolute".[29]

According to Schopenhauer, acts of compassion are intended only for the good of the object of the acts, i.e. they cannot be inspired by either the prospect of personal utility or the feeling of duty. As a result, he does not share the moral sceptic's belief that all actions of moral worth are self-interested or egoistic. From the perspective of egoism, only jurisprudence and induced incentives ('sticks and carrots') can ensure moral behaviour. Due to his criticism of Kant's moral imperative or duty,[30] Schopenhauer's theory was not accepted in his day and even now it commands little attention, but it is worth revisiting for the importance he attributes to compassion. He describes the absence of all egoistic motivation as "the criterion of an action of moral worth".[31] Schopenhauer concludes that while compassion is the source of actions of moral worth, egoism is the source of morally indifferent actions, and malice is the source of morally reprehensible ones.

Even though Schopenhauer does not believe that compassion is extensive, he acknowledges its power and sees it as intrinsic to human nature. In his philosophy, compassion or denial of the ego is attained either by personal experience of great suffering leading to subsequent moral transformation or by knowledge of the essential nature of life and understanding of the world through observing the suffering of other people.[32] One sees Buddhist teachings echoed in Schopenhauer. However, the idea that compassion leads to a desire for the universal good is found not only in Buddhism, but also in Christian teachings of love. In the *Summa Theologica,* Aquinas writes: "The essence of virtue consists of the good rather than the difficult". For him, the highest moral good is characterized by effortlessness because it springs from love.[33]

In his discussion of ethical behaviour, Varela highlights the importance of ethical experts or 'wise ones'.[34] He cites Mencius (372-289 BCE), an early Confucian. In order to distinguish virtue from its semblance, Mencius identifies four kinds of human action in ascending order of excellence, of which only one (extension) manifests truly ethical behaviour. Actions arise from 1) a desire for gain, 2) a habitual response pattern, 3) the following of rules and 4) extension, which entails seeing the other in oneself. A virtuous person does not act out ethics; a virtuous person *is* wise and ethical. For Mencius, intelligence guides our actions, in harmony with the situation and not just in accordance with rules. This requires awareness and wisdom, indispensable for compassion and extension.

To quote Martin Buber, this is "the action of the human who has become whole".[35] Through attention and extension and by training over time, we have transformed ethical action into embodied behaviour. Varela believes this is possible if we allow ourselves to become unstuck from the idea of a single, centralized unitary self, thus opening up the universe before us. Varela's was "a plea for a re-enchantment of wisdom. This skilful approach to living is based on a transformation that demands nothing less than a moment-to-moment awareness of our human nature. In its full unfolding it opens up authentic caring. These are radical ideas and strong measures for the troubled times we have at hand, and the even more troubled ones we are likely to have."

Collaboration through Empathy

In an ever more complex and globalized world, our interconnection is continually reinforced. From our interdependence in global economics and finance and politics, to our interconnectedness in the natural world, from our food chains to symbiosis among living organisms, and even to quantum physics, our universe is characterized by relations of mutual dependence. Understanding this through deep reflection is a first step toward resolving our many challenges by establishing the motivation for the next step, which is collaboration. Through discernment combined with compassionate motivation, we can then act for the common good. The Dalai Lama notes that compassion reduces fear and distrust, calms the mind and enhances understanding, thus making it easier for us to exercise discernment or intelligence.[36]

Darwin's theory of evolution and survival of the fittest is often used to justify the presumption of egoism and competition. However, in later life, Darwin noticed that animals show empathy and care and reciprocity in their behaviour and writes: "Animals not only love, but desire to be loved".[37] Jeremy Rifkin[38] presents the thesis that Herbert Spencer distorted Darwin's theory in order to fit his own social agenda. Darwin came to believe that survival of the fittest is as much about cooperation, symbiosis and reciprocity as about competition. He writes that humans and animals have a "social instinct", which is a more deeply ingrained impulse than pleasure-seeking, and speaks of a coming age when humanity will stretch its social instincts and sympathetic impulses, "becoming more tender and more widely diffused until they are extended to all sentient beings".

This makes even Darwin sound Buddhist. When asked how this will come about, he responded: "[as] soon as this virtue is honoured and practised by some few of us it spreads through instruction and example to the young and eventually becomes incorporated in public opinion".[39] Varela and many others write about the potent force of example in changing action, and in recent times we have seen the positive impact on society of the selfless behaviour of Gandhi and Mandela. Good examples breed beneficial action.

E.O. Wilson's discussion of eusociality in insects confirms Darwin's position. He writes that research shows this advanced stage of social behaviour involves two steps. First, altruistic cooperation protected the nest from enemies or predators. Second, division of labour and even sacrifice in order to further the interests of the group advanced their condition through tighter group cohesion and persistence. At the human level, belonging to a tribe or a group gives people security by placing them in an environment that is less disorienting and dangerous. In our modern world, we have a system of interlocking tribes, often at odds with one another.

Wilson writes that at the beginning of this century, biologists and anthropologists focused their research on the evolution of cooperation and determined that, in human pre-history, this was achieved through a mix of responses.[40] These include status seeking, levelling of high status of individuals by the group, and punishment and retribution for deviation from norms. Each type of behaviour includes elements of both egoism and altruism. All are interlocked in cause and effect and determined through group selection. In the earlier phase, members of the same group compete with each other in a self-serving manner. In the next phase groups compete with groups, favouring cooperative social traits. Humans, because of a large working memory, have the capacity of intentionality and a unique ability to collaborate for the purpose of achieving shared goals and intentions. Regarding future action, we can deduce that our behaviour will be influenced by our determination of goals. How extensively do we view a shared destiny? At a restricted level of family and community? At the national level? Or at the level of our shared humanity or even shared universality, including nature?

While Wilson focuses on biological reasons for cooperation, Martin Hoffman writes of the psychological and sociological. He develops a similar evolutionary theme in *Empathy and Moral Development* and writes that "humans could not have survived as a species if everyone cared only about himself... People do make sacrifices for others... This adds to the quality of life and makes social existence possible."[41] He refers to Jean-Jacques Rousseau who saw children as innately good, as sensitive to others, but vulnerable to corruption by society; and to David Hume and Adam Smith for whom empathy is a necessary social bond. For Hoffman "empathy is the spark of human concern for others, the glue that makes social life possible". Caring morality, the focus of contemporary cognitive psychology, includes justice and it informs collaborative action.

Babies are believed to be born unaware that they are separate entities and eventually to develop a cognitive sense of others. Hoffman discusses the development of empathy in children and how cognition can shape four empathy-based moral affects: sympathetic distress, empathic anger, empathic feeling of injustice and guilt over inaction. A person's pro-social moral structure is internalized when he accepts and feels obligated to abide by it without regard to external sanctions. To create powerful pro-social motives, parents need actively to socialize the child to consider others through discipline and inductions, i.e. letting the child know of disapproval for certain behaviour.

When done with care and fairness, this teaches the child empathy, a sense of justice, and responsibility for actions. It leaves the child with a sense of guilt when transgressing and the desire to make amends, but it does not provoke a sense of shame, encompassing a feeling of rejection and outrage. Such a positive feeling of guilt functions as a pro-social moral motivation. Thus, in order to cultivate empathy, discipline must be accompanied by fairness, love and nurture. Peer pressure plays an important role for it *compels* children to realize that others also have claims; cognition *enables* them to understand others' perspectives; and empathic distress and guilt *motivate* them to take others' claims and perspectives into account.

Hoffman acknowledges that this learning process does not ensure moral action, because of competing egoistic motives, but it instils an inner, compelling, moral understanding of right and wrong. To proceed from moral internalization to ethical behaviour, compassion is required. Here the giving and receiving of love is important. Hoffman believes that children who are loved are more open to the requirements of others, as compared to needy, self-absorbed children. His hypothesis is that empathy gives a potent reinforcement to abstract moral principles which lack motivating force, when they are learned in didactic contexts such as lectures and sermons. Thus, empathy activates moral principles and is reinforced by reciprocity. Hoffman's conclusion is that humans are empathic, with a disposition toward altruism, even if not naturally altruistic.

Hoffman compares his approach to empathy with John Rawls's arrival at justice through the 'difference principle', which looks at how society's least advantaged are treated.[42] Rawls uses a 'veil of ignorance' to rule out empathy, so that justice is arrived at through purely rational means. However, Hoffman argues that empathy and the veil of ignorance, though they work in different ways, one empathetically and the other rationally, have the same end result: justice. Hoffman emphasizes that "if caring and justice are valued in our society and children are socialized to internalize them both... [then] mature, morally internalized individuals have empathy-charged caring and justice principles in their motive system".[43] This perspective is similar to the inner motivation discussed by Aristotle, Aquinas, the Dalai Lama, Schopenhauer and Varela.

It is worth examining further how we internalize a moral system through the work of Antonio Damasio, the neuroscientist.[44] He shares the view that moral behaviour can be honed to the point of becoming 'second nature' if the process begins in early childhood. He emphasizes the interaction between the biological and the cultural (nature and nurture) in bringing about moral action. Through consciousness, the brain is connected to the body via feeling, and through this, we arrive at knowledge, history and culture. He differentiates between three selves: the primordial self feels pain and pleasure; the core self drives action; and the autobiographical self encompasses the social and the spiritual. This latter self gathers knowledge and guides reflective deliberation, leading through questions about the origin and purpose of life to the formation of myths, the establishment of social conventions and rules, and the enactment of moral action. He writes that "pro-moral behaviours such as kin altruism and reciprocal altruism" are innate and exhibited even long before the emergence of consciousness and reflection.

The complex evolutionary process, as described by Damasio, begins with life regulation (homeostasis) in unicellular living creatures. At a higher level, socio-cultural homeostasis enables advanced social and political systems; it is created and guided by the reflective conscious mind. It enables survival and deliberately seeks wellbeing; and it is guided by memory. Feeling allows it to imagine both individual wellbeing and the compounded wellbeing of a whole society and to invent ways and means of achieving and magnifying wellbeing. At the high level of the conscious mind, when imbalances caused by damaging social behaviour are detected, the 'homeostatic impulse' allows for the elaboration of moral rules and laws and the development of justice systems to correct the imbalance. The wisdom for such action is found in socio-cultural narratives, or storytelling, such as myths.

Damasio writes: "Building a mind capable of encompassing one's lived past and anticipated future, along with the lives of others added to the fabric and a capacity for reflection to boot, resembles the execution of a symphony of Mahlerian proportions". Biology and culture may be separate, but interactive. Damasio points to evidence that over a number of generations, cultural developments lead to changes in the genome. Thus, biology affects culture and vice versa. While the execution of moral actions becomes more and more automatic, performed to a considerable degree under non-conscious control, the decision to undertake moral behaviour and to practise one's moral skills is a very conscious and reasoned decision.[45] In choice, Damasio emphasizes the importance of reflection, as increasingly do other neuroscientists.

Ethical behaviour is further interpreted by the philosopher Paul Ricoeur through the seeing of oneself in the other.[46] He writes that because humans are intertwined, understanding the other as a mirror of the self and responsibility as a response to another's need, as well as a reaffirmation of human stature, is a necessary step towards collaboration. The ethical life is profoundly relational. He envisages just action as a response to the cry of the fragile; we start to act responsibly when we hear the cry. The necessary work ends when the cry stops; in other words, when the need for responsibility ends. We live in a world where the cry is loud and pervasive on many levels: political, economic, social and environmental. Responsible acts born of compassion are needed: they allow us to grow in human stature, providing us with a chance for self-actualization. Thus, at a deep level they do not entail sacrifice.

John Stuart Mill believes that once general happiness is recognized as the ethical standard, this will constitute the strength of morality. The desire to be in unity with our fellow human beings and to act accordingly will tend to strengthen as civilization advances. Proposing collective and not individual interest as the social aim will strengthen ties and lead to humans identifying their feelings more and more with the common good. Such a society will allow for the interests of all to be considered in collaboration. Empathy is contagious and, with the influence of education, this concept of human life will grow to be increasingly accepted, especially as sources of opposition of interest are removed.[47] This is in agreement with Darwin's view of human social connection and expansion of good behaviour through emulation.

Thus, we see empathy, ethically responsible behaviour and common purpose as the foundations for collaboration. The state has the greatest capacity to respond to the needs of society and responsibility to guarantee the *capabilities* required for human flourishing.[48] But the state can ensure the common good of its citizens only if every citizen has done his part. The civil virtue of individuals, acting out of personal choice, completes the work of government. Collaborative action begins at the level of the immediate circle of family and friends and extends beyond that to the community and the state and onto the global and universal level, based on the link that unites us all, our shared humanity. The need for global collaboration is evident, in the face of enormous problems that extend beyond any one nation's capacity to resolve them: the economic challenge and inequality, the financial crisis, the climate challenge, problems of corruption, politics and terrorism, and the cyber and technological threat. We need to start at the local level by understanding the effect of our own actions, but we cannot remain in the silo of limited impact. We must go beyond immediate problems to systemic problems and to universal problems, including nature. All are interconnected. Enhanced consciousness and empathy arrived at through attention leads to collaboration. In today's complex and challenged world, we must perforce go beyond aggressive competition to universal collaboration.

Understanding True Self-Interest

The Dalai Lama distinguishes between two forms of self-interest: 'foolish selfish' and 'wise selfish'. The former entails pursuing our self-interest in a narrow, short-sighted way. "Being wise selfish means taking a broader view and recognizing that our own long-term individual interest lies in the welfare of everyone. Being wise selfish means being compassionate."[49] The Dalai Lama is using language that we understand, the language of selfishness, in order to lead us out of selfishness. In a similar way, we can evolve self-interest the way it is normally understood, i.e. maximizing our own welfare without regard for the other's welfare, to 'enlightened' or *true self-interest*, i.e. the common good. Whether we are dealing with our own person, with economics and finance or with the environment, the key words are a broader view and long-term welfare. A narrow view of self-interest may bring about our individual desired goal in a short-lived way, but it may backfire in the long run, as we have seen with the financial and environmental crises. Only the vision that goes beyond our immediate self to the universe at large and encompassing nature can ensure true wellbeing over time. This requires compassion, a "precious inner resource, and the foundation of our wellbeing and the harmony of our societies".[50]

Compassion is discovered through experience and intelligence, but also importantly through awareness arrived at through meditation or reflection. We have discussed how contemplation helps us to arrive at true knowledge, for no knowledge is complete without two parts: *ratio* or reason and *intellectus* or contemplation.[51] We need reason to understand the world around us. But deep understanding requires awareness, which is attained through contemplation or meditation, through paying attention, through reflection. Even in the world of neuroscience, we have seen the importance of attention and reflection in the above discussion.

Compassion leads to ethical behaviour which enables the human good. It allows us to see responsibility or self-command not as sacrifice but as an act of human dignity. Thus, compassion enables virtue and virtue enables collaboration. Buckminster Fuller, who was fully aware of our environmental and social challenges, writes that the continued existence of the human species depends on wisdom, comprehensive information, integrity, collaboration and action "motivated not by crowd emotionalism or overwhelming power, but by individual conviction".[52] This conviction is arrived at through reflection; guided by compassion, we can then understand true self-interest, which is needed to ensure our survival and wellbeing.

Chapter 6

Love: The Infinite Resource

"The day you love that which is out of yourself,
on that day you will learn to love."
Friedrich Nietzsche

"Love is the highest human truth, and truth gives the fullness of life."
Rabindranath Tagore

"Only a philosophy of freedom and love can account for our existence."
Hans Urs von Balthasar

Perspectives on Love
The Human Perspective
Secular Spirituality
Love as Experience Lived
Love in Action
***Agape* and Beauty**
Network of Love

From compassion, we progress to love, one of the most widely used words in our vernacular. Many people dismiss it for this reason. Its many connotations, confusing any discussion, extend from warmth to ecstasy in emotional terms and even to pain, if love eludes our desire. However, love is more than emotion or feeling. In this chapter we turn to a holistic concept of love and attempt to recover its essence, that of love as the "ground of our being",[1] in order to explore how indispensable it is to a life well lived and to a society that functions well. Regardless of our religious beliefs or cultural background, love is the unifying essence. It is our infinite resource, for love engenders joy and joy replenishes love. Working in conjunction with power, love results in justice, the prevailing virtue. A network of love can lead to a better world of which many dream.

Perspectives on Love

The Greeks had several definitions for love that C.S. Lewis takes up in his book, *The Four Loves.* The unconditional love of family is felt through affection. It includes the need-love of the child and the gift-love of the mother, who receives love in return. Affection extends to encompass other people within our immediate circle and it is mutually satisfying. C.S. Lewis calls it the "humblest love".[2] Next, friendship or *philia* was for the Greeks "the crown of life and the school of virtue". They valued friendship highly because it permits the space within which to practise virtue and to attain happiness. We choose friendship freely. It is not imposed. *Philia* involves reciprocity; it is cultivated on both sides and demands the best in us.

When speaking of love, we often think of *eros*. In our vernacular, *eros* relates generally to the sexual and not to a deep sentiment for the beloved through which we become united. C.S. Lewis refers to it as the "state of being in love" and notes that sexual activity does not necessarily involve *eros.* The ultimate love is *agape* or charity, which is love offered without any expectation in return. This can be seen as divine love, and C.S. Lewis writes that divine love permits us not only to love God but each other. Augustine (354-430) refers to God as love, received through grace. Hannah Arendt in her study of Augustine determines that his philosophy is both outside of the world and yet involves it. In other words, in communing with the divine, a person engages fully with the world. In loving God, we love the other. Arendt began her research into love by posing a question about "the relevance of the neighbour".[3] Love is the foundation of human relations.

We usually refer to these four definitions of love as if they were separate kinds of love, but in fact they are interdependent and stem from the same source within us. Without the experience of affection, it is difficult to offer friendship. Without friendship and affection, true *eros* cannot be attained. We recall that *eros* is not sexual activity alone but union through love. And the ultimate love, *agape,* is what encapsulates all forms of love and that links us not only to the divine but to our neighbour. It is the gateway to the universal whole.

In our world, love has become banal, weakened and compromised, as the philosopher Jean-Luc Marion says: "We no longer have the words to speak of it, nor the concepts to think about it, nor the strength to celebrate it".[4] He attempts to return to the concept of love an understanding of its potent force and centrality. Marion redefines the human being not simply as the thinking person (*ego cogitans*) but as the loving being (*ego amans*), one who needs to love and to be loved. Love *is* the human essence. Although we experience love through the ego via feeling, it is not egoistical or possessive. Marion writes that "there is only one single proof of love – to give without return or chance of recovery... But love itself is never lost, because it is accomplished in loss."[5] In other words, we cannot truly love if we hold onto our ego and 'possess' love. Love is attained only through total giving, without any ulterior motive. We find love when we give love magnanimously, without expectation of return. Love is not a possession to be hoarded but a gift to be shared.

This vision is quite different from that of Dennis Robertson, an English economist of the early 20th century, who posed the question: "What do economists economize on?"[6] His answer: love. He sees love as the "most precious thing in the world" and the rarest of resources; therefore, it should not be wasted. It is to be shared only with our most intimate circle; otherwise, we risk depleting it. This perspective of love is quite different from Marion's. According to Marion, rather than being economized, love should be generously given for love replenishes love. We can thus perceive love not only as the most precious resource, but as the only resource that is infinite. Although economics concerns itself with optimizing resources, it does not discuss love, other than within the context of love of money. In fact, the discussion of love elicits ridicule and embarrassment when raised in our material world. And yet economists prize resources. Then why not love, an infinite resource?

The Human Perspective

Pitirim Sorokin worked extensively with the phenomenon of love. Having founded the Department of Sociology at the University of Harvard in 1930 and the Harvard Research Centre in Creative Altruism in the late 1940s, he studied long-term shifts in cultural patterns, as civilization moved from one ethos to another.[7] His research led him to predict that the next cultural phase will involve moral transformation through love. He writes that there are no fixed laws to cultural change as people themselves determine the over-riding ethos and value system. Human behaviour is the unknown. In his studies of monastic society in medieval times, which introduced the first orphanages, schools, hospitals, asylums, relief agencies for the needy, and banks, and which preserved art and culture, Sorokin attributes these advancements to moral transformation through love.[8] He writes that up to the 13th century the 'spiritual' (ideational) culture predominated.

The 'sensate' or 'material' culture followed, with a focus on science and technology, and this remains today. Our society has a worldly orientation towards life, with an emphasis on freedom, self-expression, material security, upward mobility, consumption, entertainment and recreation. In reviewing the concept of liberty, an important foundation of our society as already discussed, Sorokin determines that it is used to justify an incessant struggle for a larger share of material wealth and pleasure: "The more one has the more one wants".[9] However, sensate happiness is elusive and ultimately self-defeating. Sorokin recognizes that the desire for material advancement has helped the cause of individual and civil liberties and welfare. The danger is that society can become so absorbed in the desire for goods and pleasures that this overwhelms the civic spirit necessary to maintain a stable and decent society. Unbridled greed has a demoralizing and disintegrating effect upon the cohesiveness of society by weakening integrity and leading to corruption. In our financial world, but not only there, we have seen this manifested.[10]

In his study, Sorokin predicts that as people eventually become disenchanted with the material, they will long for an uplifting vision, inspired by philosophy and art. This will lead to the 'idealistic' culture, infusing the spiritual and intuitive into the material, thus enabling a complete picture of human reality. Sorokin states that a most urgent need is the humanization of society through love, thus permitting the person to assume the wellbeing of the world as his own. Dostoyevsky shares this view in *The Brothers Karamazov*: "Seeing the sins of men, one sometimes wonders whether one should react to them by force or by humble love. Always decide to fight them by humble love. If it is carried through, the whole world can be conquered".[11]

Sorokin concludes that one of the most important factors in the moral uplift of people is example, such as that of Jesus, Buddha, Confucius, St. Francis and Gandhi, which can strike the imagination and call forth mimesis and catharsis in the masses. Its effect flows not through power, force or wealth, but by the example of dedication to the highest form of love. "The emergence of one hero of love is more important than the publication of thousands of utilitarian, hedonistic and rational books on ethics."[12] This is perhaps why news columnists and commentators and the world in general are enthralled by Pope Francis, who has managed to refocus our attention on our humanity and the essential role of love. Many think he has the potential not only to change the Catholic Church for the better, but the world. His is an example the world needs.[13]

The various aspects of love described by Sorokin include the physical, the biological, the psychological, the social, the ethical, the religious and the ontological, a "unifying, integrating, harmonizing, creative energy or power".[14] This last aspect of love involves an awareness indispensable for a re-humanization of the world; it is *agape*. As we discussed in relation to compassion, love involves a meaningful interaction among people, where aspirations and aims are shared and realized in cooperation. This is the basis for a humanized economy and a harmonized world. A beneficial world order, according to Sorokin, cannot be arrived at solely through the design of institutions, important as they are, but through the "reconstruction of humanity" via moral transformation, which is the only genuine foundation of cultural change. This is more powerful than economic and political reform or new scientific discoveries.

Following Augustine, Sorokin believes that there is no one who does not love. In his empirical research on the five dimensions of love – intensity, extensity, duration, purity, and adequacy – he notes that the intensity of love diminishes as it spreads out across a greater area (extensity). Likewise, it diminishes with time (duration). Sorokin then asks how one explains the deep deposit of love in figures like St. Francis and Gandhi, and he concludes that for some this comes via intense and pure love from family, friends and companions, and for others this is received through mystical experience or transcendental love. We can deduce from this discussion that deep love gives further power to love. There is a mimetic quality to love. The more love is practised, the more it is returned. The purer it is, the more intense it is and the longer its duration. Sorokin contrasts this with 'soiled' love, based on selfish, utilitarian and hedonistic motivations, which is weak and not lasting. In fact, by love's true definition, this is not love.

How then can we attain the deep reservoir of love that can help reform the world? Sorokin agrees with Martin Hoffman's conclusion that love received in early life predisposes one to love.[15] Some discover love through encounter with another who personifies love. Some come to love through a deep awakening after suffering a disastrous and tragic experience.[16] We can arrive at love through joy or suffering. Instead of the common view that suffering leads to frustration and provokes aggression,[17] he believes that suffering can lead to love through opening us up to a deeper awareness. At a deep level, love transcends.

Sorokin discusses moral transformation, such as sacramental rituals, prayer, meditation (attention through mindfulness) and uplifting art. Stillness of the mind helps to transcend the ego, unleashing love. Affiliations, particularly family links, reinforce altruistic love. Through love and attention, we attain 'integral knowledge', understanding the interconnectedness of things. Sorokin was writing in the 1950s, in a period of rising materialism when such metaphysical discussion was looked at askance. Despite his status, his observations were not given due consideration and gradually forgotten. However, in recent times, neuroscientists, psychologists, physicists and philosophers have written in support of the primacy of love. We have discussed some of them, including Francisco Varela, the neuroscientist. He said in an interview: "Love is the manifestation of two things: intelligence and profound empathy". Intelligence is not necessarily a high intelligence quotient or IQ. It implies wisdom. It is an awareness of the world around us and its interrelatedness.

Secular Spirituality

Luc Ferry, the contemporary French philosopher and ex-Minister of Education, shares Sorokin's belief that love will become an important force in shaping society. He writes that love, which gives meaning to our existence, can become the foundation for a new vision of the world. He calls it the 'revolution of love' or 'secular spirituality', a new humanism.[18] He predicts that love - friendship and fraternity - will form the new binding force for society, in response to three developments in our times: 1) the breakdown of traditional values in the search for individual expression,[19] leading to a highly permissive capitalistic society; 2) impotency of individual governments in the face of a complex global system; and 3) paradoxically, a re-enchantment with the world discovered through globalization, leading to a new awareness of our interconnectedness. In the first case, we try to compensate for the disintegration of a rich interior life with unbridled and frenetic consumption, endlessly seeking new experience. This frenetic search causes a further disintegration of moral order, as material goods are sought at any price.

Ferry argues that the philosophy of love stems from the need for a new moral order. The Enlightenment was characterized by Immanuel Kant's categorical imperative, of dutiful attention to the common good or what Kant called 'universality'. It required a certain goodwill and 'self-detachment', without focus on individual interest, and it ensured a cohesive moral force. When this order broke down, extreme egoism, hedonism and hyper-consumption followed. In line with our preoccupation in this book, it is in response to the dehumanization of the world through the advance of senseless consumption, brute capitalism and destruction wrought by the excesses of finance, that Ferry believes a new humanism is in order. He sees an urgent need to return sense and value to our lives. Increasingly we recognize that despite differences in culture and backgrounds, humans share basic values and aspirations, such as honesty, responsibility, justice and a desire for love and happiness.

Enlightenment philosophy, which placed the human being at the centre of the universe, was founded on two pillars: reason and liberty. Ferry argues that this philosophy lacks an important consideration, wisdom. Philosophy, as the study of wisdom, highlights the importance of living a life that has meaning. A 'good life' is lived through meaning. Here Ferry returns to the Aristotelian concept of a 'life well lived' and of virtue seen not simply as the struggle against human weakness, but as the actualization of natural human potential. The focus on Cartesian logic[20] has made us forget wisdom. While the Age of Reason and the scientific revolution brought many benefits, they have also weakened our intuitive faculty and spiritual depth. Ferry proposes that we recover wisdom through a new moral vision, where fraternal love permeates all interactions and provides substance to civic and political action. In this way we reinforce the traditional 'fraternity' of 'solidarity', of which the State is the final guarantor, as well as offer a response to the complex challenges that the State appears impotent to resolve. The motivating force for this enriched vision is love for justice, nature, truth and our fellow humans. Ferry writes: "The love of wisdom leads to the wisdom of love".

He calls this proposed new order the 'second humanism', characterized not simply by rights and reason, but also by love, a regard for the other. This important principle of love is integrated into that of liberty and reason. Morality above all is respect for the other and entails generosity and goodwill. Responsibility entails choosing action for the common good. The Stoics differentiated between what can and what cannot be controlled. Through our control over moral choice, we can influence for the good the future of the world, the course of which individually we do not control.

Ferry attributes the advance of the 'revolution of love' to romantic love and creation of the family unit through marriage by choice. By extension, love encompasses the collective. For secular society, he sees this as the new sacred order of transcendence in the immanent world, transcendence of the self and the other through love. An agnostic, Ferry calls it 'secular spirituality'. Love over-rides egoism. Although our current cultural vision assumes this is impossible, Ferry maintains that it *is* possible and, in fact, mandatory, if we are to repair a broken world.

It is not simply because of a utopian ideal that Ferry argues in this way. It is because the complexity of the challenges facing our world deprives government of simple policy solutions. In line with Ferry's position and in order to ensure our wellbeing, we can say that action inspired by love is vital, as well as education to reinforce it. We observe the practice of love within family and social units. We know the feeling of love that accompanies us and the state of wellbeing it elicits. We may have experienced the happiness it contributes to. Yes, love is a grace, but it is also enabled by choice. Love begets love. It infuses all and cannot be compartmentalized. It gives unity to action towards a common good. Its birth is influenced by choice.

Love as Experience Lived

Love has been celebrated in literature, music and other art forms throughout history and across civilizations. Bards sang about love, both platonic and romantic, during the Middle Ages. Love is explored not only in art, but religion, philosophy, anthropology, sociology, psychology and increasingly in neuroscience and physics. *Eros* is the moving power of life towards union. In reading Aristotle's *The Politics,* "we learn from Aristophanes in the *Erotics...*

that those who love one another from the excess of that passion, desire to breathe the same soul, and from being two to be blended into one".[21]

Some people experience a deep love with an exemplary person that is life changing. It can inspire confidence in human potential and unleash action in service of humanity or a search for divine love. All these responses reinforce the primacy of love. We discussed earlier the encounter of Auguste Comte and Clotilde de Vaux and how it reinforced his belief that duty and devotion to humanity is possible and that the good of humanity is the ultimate standard of what is right. For C.S. Lewis, the death of his beloved wife Joy led to a better understanding of the magnanimity of God and divine love: "We could almost say He sees because He loves, and therefore loves although He sees".[22]

Ken Wilber, known for his work on integral theory,[23] writes about the fearless strength and passionate equanimity of his wife, Treya Killam, as she battled with breast cancer before finally succumbing to it, in *Grace and Grit*. The portrayal of how she brought meditative awareness to embrace pain and dissipate its hold on her led to almost a thousand readers writing to Wilber to express what her story meant to them and how it changed their lives. This is a story of determination and joy that overcomes pain and terror. For Killam, joy came through a search for meaning via contemplative or meditative spirituality, from embracing the present. This is not simply a story of deep love lived, but the discovery of meaning through pain and a description of how suffering not avoided or denied can lead to transcendence.[24] It confirms the human promise.

John Stuart Mill advanced the idea of wealth maximization as the motivation for human behaviour, thus laying the foundation for *homo oeconomicus*. However, he became one of the most humane of economists. Influenced by his passion for his wife, Harriet Taylor, he sees happiness as deriving primarily from love, which arises not from aiming to maximize it, but by fixing on some object other than oneself and one's own happiness.[25] He believes that the ultimate happiness comes from experiencing another's happiness.

This is indeed different from the concept of utilitarianism, with which he is also associated and where happiness is maximized through pleasure in Bentham's 'felicific calculus'.

Mill's encounter with his wife, "the most admirable person" he had ever known, marked a turning point in his life and thought. Mill writes that her "passion of justice" was manifested in an "indignation at everything brutal or tyrannical, faithless or dishonourable". Moreover, "her unselfishness was not that of a taught system of duties, but of a heart which thoroughly identified itself with the feelings of others". He presents through his words a person inspired by love and a passion for life and humanity.[26] He describes theirs as "the friendship which has been the honour and chief blessing of my existence, as well as the source of a great part of all that I have attempted to do, or hope to effect thereafter, for human improvement".[27] Not only did Mill love his wife, he respected her. Respect is an indispensable component of love.

While acknowledging his own ability in the establishment of theory, Mill attributes to Harriet Taylor the development of a wise scepticism and a deepening in his understanding, particularly in "the region of ultimate aims, the constituents of the highest realizable ideal of human life". Following her death, her perceived approbation became the standard by which he endeavoured to live. She was indeed the cause of a profound metamorphosis in Mill's attitude and thinking. A younger Mill had responded with the words "sentimentality" and "vague generalities" to criticism of utilitarianism as cold calculation and political economy as hard-heartedness. He explains that "the cultivation of feeling (except the feelings of public and private duty) was not in much esteem among us, and had very little place in the thoughts of most of us, myself in particular". His objective had been to alter people's opinion through evidence and to appeal to their own interest. While recognizing the excellence of unselfish benevolence and love of justice, he had not believed in their force but rather in that of educated intellect. Thus, he had not been a man of the heart, but of reason.[28] He acknowledges that all this changed after his "complete union" with Harriet Taylor and attributes much of his later writing to her influence.

The economist Luigino Bruni writes that Mill treats the idea of the life of the couple as *agape,* that is as a reciprocal union exalting both the individuality of each partner and their complementarities. Mill was convinced that marriage is founded on friendship (the key idea of *The Subjection of Women*,[29] a thesis that places Mill among the first feminists): "There is a foundation for solid friendship, of an enduring character, more likely than anything else to make it, through the whole of life, a greater pleasure to each to give pleasure to the other, than to receive it". Solid marriage is based on "care for great objects and... help and encouragement to each other in whatever regards these".[30] Marriage, through *agape,* allows for self-actualization.

Love in Action

Just as a young John Stuart Mill had termed 'sentimental' the charge levelled at his economic theory of cold calculation and hard-heartedness, likewise do rationalists respond to any discussion of love within the political and economic realms. Love is viewed as soft and weak and power as strong and forceful. For this reason, love is ignored in politics and economics and seen as ineffective. Martin Luther King criticized the polarized definitions of love as "resignation of power" and of power as "denial of love".[31] In a speech, he said: "Power without love is reckless and abusive and love without power is sentimental and anaemic. Power at its best is love implementing the demands of justice, and justice at its best is love correcting everything that stands against love." What power was he referring to? Not the power enabled by wealth and physical strength that we normally think of, but the power of just action, effected through love.

In 1967, King called for a "revolution of values" through "an all-embracing and unconditional love for all mankind. This oft misunderstood, this oft misinterpreted concept, so readily dismissed by... the world as a weak and cowardly force, has now become an absolute necessity for the survival of man. When I speak of love I am not speaking of some sentimental and weak response. I am not speaking of that force which is just emotional bosh. I am speaking of that force which all of the great religions have seen as the supreme unifying principle of life. Love is somehow the key that unlocks the door which leads to ultimate reality."[32] King was speaking in the face of the Vietnam War and during a period when civil rights were still to be won. Today, the threat to peace remains and the challenges we face include terrorism, wars, economic and financial disintegration and environmental threats. The urgency is even greater.

In his speech, King elaborated: "If we do not act, we shall surely be dragged down the long, dark, and shameful corridors of time reserved for those who possess power without compassion, might without morality, and strength without sight". Today, we often no longer seem to feel the stigma of shame when we abuse trust. Nonetheless, many recognize the need to restore a moral order, a sense of values. For King there was a desire for a "long and bitter, but beautiful, struggle for a new world". Almost fifty years later, we continue to struggle and to see the urgent need for a "revolution of values and of love". This book concerns itself with the ethical vision or virtue born of compassion and love, a need to correct the abuses of finance and of the environment, among many other abuses. Thus, King's message of love and power, enabling justice, is potent.

Paul Tillich, a foremost theologian of the 20th century and King's professor and advisor, shows that the best way to deal with the issues of love, power and justice is to situate the discussion within ontology (the study of the nature of being).[33] He sees grounding these words in the human being as the only way to avoid the confusion that they tend to elicit. People define them differently; as a result, any cohesive discussion of them becomes problematic. It is vital to return to the essential issue, by asking in which way each of these words is grounded in its common root, the human being.

Tillich writes that emotion is embedded in the word 'love'. We associate love with feeling, but it is not simply an emotion. Love is much more. It is the moving force of life, the drive towards unity: "It is the fulfilment and the triumph of love that it is able to reunite the most radically separated beings, namely individual persons". There is no love without emotion, which Tillich attributes to the exciting anticipation of reunion. Hence, love is a passion, and fulfilled love through unification is ultimate happiness. In Christian faith, there is the commandment of love, which is manifested differently in other religions and philosophies. Tillich observes then that love has an ethical nature, which is dependent on the ontological (the state of being), because an emotion cannot be commanded. Thus, to a certain extent, we *decide* to love.

Aristotle describes *eros* as driving everything towards its highest form. The movement he describes is the realization of the potential of love. Tillich explains that this movement is enabled by power. Thus, the dynamic self-affirmation of love is power, manifested through the self-actualization of being. In the sociological realm, there is a relation of force to power, as in 'power politics'. Tillich writes: "The centre of power is only the centre of the whole as long as it does not degrade its own centrality by using it for particular purposes". In other words, legitimate power is not corrupt.

What makes power degenerative or corrupt? When there is a lack of love, a unifying purpose. Tillich argues that when power is used for an individual particular purpose opposed to that of the whole, the aim of love or reunion with the separated is prevented, thus corrupting power. With love and power united, justice results. He writes that justice is realized when people are treated as *persons* and not as *objects*. Justice is more than law. Justice has both a legal and an ethical aspect, and it has a creative dynamic through love. It can be reached only if both the demands of the universal law and of the particular situation are met. In discussing Plato, Tillich highlights that for him justice is the unifying form of the individual and the social body. Justice enables the individual to live in unity with society.

By setting love, power and justice within an ontological framework, Tillich makes the ethical discussion one that concerns the nature of the human being. If we see it like this, we recognize ethics as fundamental to our existence, and not subject to relativist interpretations according to culture, biology or psychology. Tillich sees ethics not as ideals that *ought to be* according to values we assign, but as what *is*. This is a very powerful argument for ethical behaviour. He also places love prominently within human action that is just. Love is the clearest way to arrive at self-actualization of the human being, and justice is the path.

Thich Nhat Hanh, the Vietnamese Buddhist monk and peace activist, has a similar understanding. He writes that "the essence of non-violence is love".[34] It is to understand that if we harm another person or nature, we harm ourselves. Non-violence is not dogma or a simple adherence to the law, but a process born of the awareness of suffering and nurtured through love. He believes in the primal goodness born of love in every individual, and he writes that power is born from awareness and self-control.[35] Awareness comes from meditation or reflection on knowledge, leading to wisdom and good action. The ultimate power is realized through joy, peace and unity, not through obtaining the exclusive benefit of something or by depriving another of that benefit. The ultimate power is love in action.

Agape and Beauty

For the ancient Greeks, *agape* represented the divine spirit, the principle of cohesion of the cosmic order, the aspiration of the world towards unity. *Agape* is the ultimate form of love, the purest love, divine love. Augustine wrote that God is love. He sought God with a heart that *believes* and an intelligence that *sees*. He was not content simply with knowing God through the intellect. He sought the experience of God, and this he found in love, in relationship. Augustine writes: "Let no one say 'I don't know what to love.' Let him love his brother, and love that Love... Embrace love which is God, and embrace God with love."[36] We cannot understand love in abstraction, but we know it through emotion and relationship, as a starting point towards transcendence.

Through contemplation of the Trinity (Father, Son and Holy Spirit), Augustine discovered the experience of love. In love or *caritas,* we find the lover, the beloved and love. Piero Coda, known for his work on Trinitarian Ontology, writes: "Love is always Trinitarian. This is obvious first of all in the love of friendship: where two souls, one who loves and the other who is loved, are united with the most sublime love"[37] that is the spirit. The encounter with God through love is not an abstraction of the intellect, nor does it simply rest at the divine level, but enters into the dynamic of life itself. St. Francis of Assisi exemplified this love through his life and gave authority to it.[38] He loved not only his fellow human beings, but nature as well: mother earth, brother sun and sister moon.[39] His love was for the whole universe.

The Jesuit mystic, Pierre Teilhard de Chardin, believes that the way humans evolve into universal consciousness is by harnessing the power of love, by "awakening the tremendous spiritual power slumbering in our midst". He writes about the evolution of consciousness to the *omega* point of supreme synthesis.[40] Psychic energy increases in complexity and intensifies until it becomes "Christic" energy, when we are in full union with Christ in love. Teilhard believes that the first phase of human evolution is towards extreme individualism and separation and the second phase towards interrelation and cooperation.[41] At the apex, the new human has gone beyond the self into integration with the other and with nature, and has transcended individuality into unity. This is the *omega* point, the fulfilment of the divine plan for creation, the *pleroma* as written by St. Paul, when the fullness of God is reached.[42] This is the movement towards union, integrating the fragmented world in which we live and giving it dignity. A scientist, Teilhard had a great respect for the earth, and his discussion of the world comprises the natural, as well as the human. Hence, he is a mystic for our environmentally and socially challenged times.

A discussion of consciousness and energy brings us into common ground with philosophies like Buddhism and that of the Chinese sages. Since Buddhism is well known to most, I will limit my brief comments to Chinese teachings. In Chinese cosmology, the primordial energy, breath or *qi* is divided into three types: the active force (*yin*), the passive force (*yang*), and median emptiness. It is through interaction of the three breaths that mutual transformation results. With *qi*, early Chinese thinkers advanced a unifying and organic concept of the universe where all is connected and held together in the *Tao*, the Way. For the Chinese, true beauty is found in the encounter between the human spirit and the living universe and allows for mutual transcendence. This is love in its most expressive form. The poet François Cheng describes the three fundamental Oriental notions for assessing a work of art: *yin-yun* (unifying interaction), *qi-yun* (rhythmic breath or energy), and *shen-yun* (divine resonance).[43] In this, we observe the unifying nature of art and beauty and the resultant transcendence.[44] For Chinese sages, love is unity, celebration and transcendence.

In line with the Greeks, the Chinese see beauty and love and ethics as intertwined.[45] Cheng writes about the two extremes in human conduct: ethics as beauty and evil as ugliness. In order to practice *ren* (virtue of humanity), Confucius (551-479 BCE) saw the necessity of *li* (ritual of just relations) and *yue* (music and poetry, beauty leading to harmony). The Greek word *kalosagathos,* which represents the ideal human conduct of harmony in mind and body, contains the idea of beauty (*kalos*) and good or virtue (*agathos*). Plato saw the true, the good and the beautiful as fundamental human aspirations. In the Romantic Age, beauty was seen as truth, as sung by John Keats: "Beauty is truth, and truth beauty".[46] Dostoyevsky is known for presenting the dark side of humankind, and yet wrote in *The Idiot* that "beauty will save the world".[47] Augustine saw beauty as representing God and love.[48] These are different representations of beauty as bringing about the good. True beauty inspires goodness and love, leading to transcendence.

Network of Love

Whether we subscribe to the idea of divine or earthly love, most of us have experienced love, and if we have the misfortune of never having known it, we most likely desire it. Augustine writes: "There is no one who does not love".[49] Christopher Hitchens, the late self-pronounced antitheist, journalist, writer and thinker, agrees with Bertrand Russell that a moment of love is worth the whole of the rest of life.[50] If we have experienced a circle of love, should we not seek to expand it? We have seen that love is a grace but also a choice, and within the Christian faith a commandment. According to Tillich, love is not simply an emotion, which cannot be commanded, but part of our being. It is in our essence and natural order.

Many may not share an all-encompassing vision of love and may agree with the philosopher Harry Frankfurt that we can only love those within the boundaries of our practical life.[51] Frankfurt looks at love not from an ontological, but from a personal perspective, which is generally the way love is perceived in our society, as encompassing our immediate world. Nonetheless, love for another will dictate beneficial action towards the beloved. By linking these various circles of love, a greater space is covered and this can grow. Luc Boltanski, the sociologist, writes that love cannot be taught or forced, but is expanded simply by creating the conditions that cause it to disseminate.[52] We germinate love, and love engenders love. It is an infinite resource, the only resource we have that is infinite.

Whether love predominates in the world depends on our choice between tribal and universal altruism. Mo-tzu (*ca.* 475-393 BCE) describes the enlarged egoism of tribal altruism: "A thief loves his own family and does not love other families, hence he steals from other families in order to benefit his own... The causes of all disturbances... lie herein... It is always from want of equal love to all."[53] Such behaviour leads to aggression and violence and revenge to those outside the tribe. Sorokin writes that these encroachments can be overcome by the extension of altruistic conduct beyond the membership of one's group to all humans, by a "network of love".[54]

This extension need not imply an equal distribution of love among all people. The initial stages of this process require first that each loves the members of his family and immediate circle of friends. If everyone does so, each member of the human race will find himself loving and being loved by someone, with no member of the universe unloved and not loving. This may appear idealistic and naive, for hard circumstances give some people no chance for love in life. It may be so, but an extended network of love may mitigate the harshness of such circumstance and even turn arid ground into a fruitful one. In *The Grapes of Wrath*, John Steinbeck writes of migrants, leaving the dust belt in Oklahoma for California in search of jobs, finding solace in each other and building a network of support.[55]

A network of love also implies that everyone abstains from action wilfully harmful to another. Moreover, it means that everyone, within his capacity, extends a loving hand to those in need of help and sympathy, firstly within his immediate community, and eventually spreading through the whole of humanity. The more people participate in this network, the easier the work becomes. Sorokin writes: "Hate begets hate, violence engenders violence, hypocrisy is answered by hypocrisy, war generates war, and love creates love".

To promote love, competition can be redirected from serving conflicts to encouraging creativity. Competition can showcase accomplishment, rather than celebrate the defeat of another.[56] Through a network of love, each person contributes to building altruistic responses and extends friendly conduct beyond their tribe to all of humanity, thus enabling peace. Such a transformation must perforce come from the individual; it starts at the grassroots and within communities and expands from there. Behaviour is guided by education and observation, and awareness is enhanced through reflection. Love is not sentimental bosh. It is the powerful glue of society and the common ground of philosophy and religion that can unite the world. We live and expand love through action, by living love.

Integration

Money, Love and Virtue: Humanism

"The prophet and the poet may regenerate the world without the economist, but the economist cannot regenerate it without them."
Philip Wicksteed

"All economic change is a change in the economic community, a change in the community's methods of turning material things to account. The change is always in the last resort a change in habits of thought."
Thorstein Veblen

"Only the idea which has materialized in the flesh can influence man; the idea which remains a word only changes words."
Erich Fromm

Reflection
Abstract Theory or Human Concern?
The Timeless Social Contract
Blossoming of Society: Humanism
Language and Landscape are Shifting
Amoral, Immoral, or Ethical?
Expanding an Imagined Ideal

~~~

Reflection

I have offered a brief review of the history of economic and social thought, in order to see how our ideas about the economy and the uses of money have developed. What is the purpose of the economy and money? Since both were originally meant to serve human beings and society at large, classical thinking on civil organization and the social contract has been helpful in assessing our current ways of organizing ourselves.

The way we organize society reflects our assumptions, prejudices, and beliefs, so I have reflected first on the extent to which our view of the human being affects things, favourably or not. The Freudian concept of the person mired in his ego is being challenged by a more positive view of the social human being, linked to and having a regard for the other. The idea that it is permissible to talk about empathy, compassion and even love is gaining ground across disciplines and beginning to influence academic discourse. In this context, collaboration, rather than competition, is important. With a positive view of the person gradually entering our social
~~~

consciousness, perhaps we can move forward towards realization of our human potential and the common good.

Some may think I have covered too much ground or too disparate topics, and perhaps not sufficiently rigorously. But this is not an academic study. It is a *reflection*. I have found it necessary to take such a broad approach because I believe we have to look at the way in which things are interconnected in order to understand how they affect our lives. Specialization abounds, but the intricacy of our human condition is complex. So I have explored three central concepts that affect our lives – money, love and virtue – in an attempt to understand that intricacy.

My reflection stems from a concern about economic and financial issues, as this is the area of my professional interest and experience, and within the realm of economic and financial management, a great debate is taking place about what its future course should be. However, great challenges confront us in many areas. With an expanding population, particularly outside the Western world, and in the face of environmental threats, the effective management of our resources (both financial and environmental) becomes more pressing. Scarcity threatens peace, but that is not the only threat. Increasingly we see different cultural goals, social visions and religious beliefs conflicting with one another. Moreover, fast changing technology will have an impact on all aspects of our lives.

In such a world, facing the possibility of seismic change at many levels, we need more than ever to comprehend the intricacies of overlapping issues, ideas and actions that determine our world and shape our lives. And we need to intervene. In order to respond to these challenges in a peaceful way that will serve us all, we have to call upon our humanity.

Abstract Theory or Human Concern?

With the advent of the scientific age, there came a desire to validate economics by turning it into a science. As the world became increasingly complex and extended, abstraction and theory were thought to provide the answer to economic questions and to offer a map for improving human welfare. Leading economists like Friedrich Hayek argued that, in small social groupings, human relationships can advance the understanding of economic behaviour, but in large, anonymous societies like ours, this is neither practical nor feasible. Profit then becomes the means by which we measure and achieve economic outcome. Hayek maintained that making a profit is in fact an act of altruism in an abstract and extended society, as it results in our serving people we do not know and who live beyond our immediate awareness.[1] This was his understanding of self-interest and the invisible hand.

We have seen that Hayek's view of profit has not been borne out. Rather, abstraction and theory have distanced economics – which is so intimately linked to the human condition – from overall human wellbeing, and led to its losing sight of our deeper purpose. John Stuart Mill recognized in later life his mistake in assuming the acquiring of monetary wealth to be the sole motivation for human behaviour and highlighted the role of love, which lies at our core.

The development of mathematical modelling has also influenced the course of finance, with a resultant impact on human society. It has been used to delineate the most efficient use of money. The measure of efficiency is maximization of return in business and portfolio management. This is the yardstick for measuring whether money is well employed. Because a specific idea of self-interest as discussed is widely accepted, the owner of financial assets tends to seek to maximize his own return without any regard for external consequences – be they environmental, social or even economic – on society at large. Immediate or short-term maximization of financial return takes precedence over the long term. With technological advance, the tools used to enhance returns facilitated speculation, further increasing the risk of damage to the financial and economic edifice.

While financial theory may be abstract, financial behaviour is not. It affects the financial system and subsequently the economy and, therefore, it has human consequences. Because finance links all parts of the economy, thus impacting on society, no action can be assessed without consideration of its effect on the whole. In order to take responsibility in finance, we must understand the financial and economic framework and its impact. After all, money is the life-blood of society. A central question is: how can money be well used and to what extent does the reckless pursuit of money cause damage?

The purpose of finance must be properly understood and aligned with human needs. If finance is to benefit society at large, it must lead to the creation of sustainable wealth. Finance is a tool for economic management, a vital one. As the purpose of finance is to enable a flourishing economy, it has to serve the human community. How can finance allow the economy to thrive? By providing it with the tools to achieve human progress. Finance is a means to provide investment, innovation, sustainable growth and true prosperity.[2]

Wealth creation achieved via money games and speculative plays will have to give way to prosperity achieved via investment and spending that benefit society. This will include investing wisely in technology and biotechnology. And there are investment needs for infrastructure spending and transitioning to a sustainable economy. As big as, if not bigger than our financial problem, is the environmental challenge we face,[3] to which we have not devoted much discussion. It is gratifying that sustainable investment, which takes environmental considerations into account, is gaining attention. Long-term sustainable investment, which provides avenues for innovation, can build a better future. Intoxicating perks arising from speculative short-term trades or real estate flips do not. Society is best served by a financial framework that can support the economy now and into the distant future.

The short-termism of investors was already of concern to John Maynard Keynes in the 1930s. He acknowledged the merits of a long-term approach and opined that "decisions affecting the future... cannot depend on strict mathematical expectations, since the basis for such calculation does not exist" and that "enterprise which depends on hopes stretching into the future benefits the community as a whole".[4] He was warning us that blind confidence in mathematical forecasting is misplaced and planning a better future requires the input of more than numbers. It requires hope and human aspiration. In order to serve us, finance has to incorporate the human dimension. It must be accompanied by consideration for others and by self-command. It cannot exclude love and virtue.

The Timeless Social Contract

Money should comply with the social contract, which is one of the foundations of civilization. The social contract aims to provide the conditions for society at large to meet its material requirements and realize human aspirations and to survive in peace and harmony. For John Locke, the two pillars of self-preservation are property or wealth and civic action or trust. An arch cannot be held up without two pillars. Similarly, the social contract collapses without trust. Investment is a way to acquire wealth and must incorporate trust and a view to the future. Locke highlights regard for the other and a sense of unity; he sees society as a living body. He emphasizes the common good.

Adam Smith's economic synthesis upholds liberty, another key component of the social contract. Wealth permits liberty, as one is not subject to the whim of another. One need not beg. Liberty enables equality in a marketplace, thereby facilitating exchange if transactions take place in a context of fairness and trust, in reciprocity and friendship. Each agent benefits from the transaction. Self-command must perforce accompany self-interest if the invisible hand is to function. All three need to be present for the common good to result. Smith's understanding of self-interest is not egoistical, but includes regard for the other and for the consequences of action. In our times, without self-command, wealth distribution has become skewed and the invisible hand ineffective.

Machiavelli did not propose simply deceit and manipulation, as some readers of *The Prince* would have us believe. Inspired by the

Roman republican ideal of Livy, Machiavelli writes that a city can only be great if the good of the community is placed above private interest in a society within which liberty is sacrosanct and the law indispensable. Civic action comprises both human behaviour and institutional organization. As members of society, we must live within the law and with our institutions. To ensure beneficial outcomes, they too must be well designed.

Even with the most perfect laws and institutions, the social contract works only with good citizens. While John Rawls stresses freedom, law and the perfect institution,[5] Aristotle emphasizes virtue as a way to justice, a foundation for a good society. Paul Tillich writes that justice is the union of power and love, as well as union of the individual with the social body. Therefore, along with virtue, love or friendship is an important component of the social contract. With love, the person is other-regarding and possesses virtue, expressed in self-command.

Blossoming of Society: Humanism

In order to be potent, the motivation for a virtuous or ethical life must arise from within, and not simply be imposed through external rules. Inner motivation stems from compassion or love. This view of virtue does not imply that it is a burden or that it requires sacrifices that will restrict freedom. Rather it is the path to a flourishing life that is fully human, permitting a humanistic society, one that recognizes the civil function of the economy and money. The organizing principles of such a society are friendship or reciprocity, consideration and collaboration, with the human being at the centre. Liberty permits freedom and prosperity for the individual, but true liberty can only exist if a person's liberty mirrors that of the other, if it does not intrude on the other's liberty but instead respects the other.

We are interconnected social beings. The biologist E.O. Wilson describes biological evolution resulting in greater cooperation and even altruism, while the neuroscientist Antonio Damasio gives a neurological explanation of how the reflective conscious mind, as guided by feeling, corrects socially damaging behaviour. He writes that this process makes possible advanced social and political systems through the elaboration of moral rules and laws and the development of systems of justice. A functioning social system requires both reason and compassion .

Providing a sociological view of history, Pitirim Sorokin establishes that an early spiritual culture was replaced by a material culture. He predicts that, arising from our disenchantment with the material, a new culture infusing the spiritual and the intuitive into the material will eventually lead to an idealistic culture that will serve the total needs of all humans. In a similar vein, Teilhard de Chardin describes a spiritual vision of the evolution of consciousness to an *Omega* point of love. So we see different perspectives all suggesting a living body composed of our separate selves, as described by John Locke. The desired goal is unity and harmony, or what Aristotle calls the good life: *eudaimonia* or happiness.

In order to attain this goal, Martha Nussbaum suggests that we rethink Enlightenment principles in the present-day context, so as to offer a civil approach to the good life. She believes that humanism and universalism offer a contemporary understanding of equality and fraternity:[6] together they nurture human dignity and engage empathy and global citizenship. She notes that stewardship of nature is part of this consideration. In this book we have discussed virtue, which equates to global citizenship, and love, which equates to empathy. Nussbaum suggests that liberty can be seen as autonomy, the capacity to express oneself. But autonomy does not mean self-expression without restraint. Self-examination may help us realize that our wants may not always be in accordance with our needs. Michael Sandel reinforces this civic approach, which is respectful of the other.

In order to agree on a shared destiny, we must ask ourselves what kind of world we would like to live in, for together we define the world. We need to remind ourselves of the belief of the Stoics: we may not control the world, but we can control our own behaviour and through it influence the course of events and history. Good citizenship or virtuous action is a matter of choice and it is a capacity that resides in every one of us. Humanism is inspired by enlightened self-interest and love for the common good, which includes the totality of public commodities and services, but also something more profound and more human. It includes the sum of our civic conscience, or virtue. And *philia*, friendship or love, enables virtue; both are intertwined.

Language and Landscape are Shifting

The marriage of money, love and virtue may seem obscure in today's world – even though, as we have seen, they have been intricately intertwined in thinking about society and justice since ancient times. The language we use to speak about the world of economics and finance is changing and, as a result, the world may eventually be transformed. Words and ideas that would have been considered foreign to business and finance are now debated by the most privileged 1% and used even by the Governor of the Bank of England. They include morals, the social contract, intergenerational equity and justice. Mark Carney, at a conference in 2014 on inclusive capitalism, criticized market ideology and said that "when belief in the power of the market enters the realm of faith"[7] it can devour the social capital that is essential for the long-term dynamism of capitalism. He attributes the financial crisis to this blind faith. Along with Michael Sandel, he acknowledges that our move from a market economy to a market society has had detrimental effects.

In the *McKinsey Quarterly* of September 2014, Eric Beinhocker and Nick Hanauer offer a redefinition of capitalism under attack.[8] Their article leads us to ask whether corporate social responsibility, previously relegated to the margins and mainly exploited for marketing purposes, will finally become mainstream and fully integrated into corporate policy and strategy.[9] The authors acknowledge that capitalism has led to the spread of prosperity in the West in the 19th and 20th centuries and in emerging countries in the recent past. Nonetheless, conventional economic theories have not given us a full understanding of its workings. The view that markets and prices lead to an efficient allocation of resources has proven faulty. Neither is human behaviour rational nor markets perfect. Instead, "the economy – a complex, dynamic, open and nonlinear system – has more in common with an ecosystem than with the mechanistic systems that neo-classicists modelled their theory on". The authors conclude that the real contribution of markets is in promoting creativity and, hence, "the essential role of capitalism is not allocation – it is creation". Capitalism provides incentives for "solving human problems" and it is these solutions that define prosperity, not money.

The authors argue that such an approach would move the objective away from short-term profit maximization to long-term investment. A redefinition of GDP should then incorporate a measurement of new solutions and their availability represented across a basket of goods. This proposal may represent a step forward, but a related and unanswered question is this: how are the problems defined and how are they solved? Do solutions bring benefit to some but adversely affect others? What is their impact on nature? In response, the authors would argue that democracy and regulation help guide us along this path. But how are citizens best served? It is not necessarily by having more options in relation to goods and services and more avenues for pleasure. Nor is it by having complex legislation that provides loopholes for contravention. To arrive at true creativity to resolve our complex human organization, we need reflection as well as reason, *intellectus* as well as *ratio*. We must understand the human condition and our interconnectedness. We require love and virtue.

Education can reinforce civic behaviour and influence cultural reform. While profit maximization is still taught at business schools, students are increasingly calling for curricular reform in order better to understand financial impact and environmental and social considerations, such as inequality.[10] In this context, economic and management theory will eventually evolve.[11] Ethics is being re-introduced at business schools and finding its way back onto university curricula. Alfred Marshall supposedly said: "Every university must consider from time to time whether its scheme of study and teaching is adequate to current needs". In his time, the need was to confirm economics as a science. The Industrial Revolution required tools for enhancing efficiency, as production methods were being transformed, allowing for mass production to lift many out of deprivation and misery. Today we live in a paradoxical world. We have scarcity in the midst of plenty. Perhaps now is the time to reintroduce into economics a consideration of wisdom, of philosophy, which is where the study of economics began. Keynes said that an economist must be "mathematician, historian, statesman and philosopher".[12]

Following the 2008 financial crisis, it was suggested that the public be educated in financial principles and management, so that they might make better decisions and avoid falling into traps. It is indeed necessary and useful to teach people to improve money management and avoid the waste of a valuable resource. However, it is not only the investment public that must be educated. Agents in the financial world also need to understand the ramifications of their actions. In order fully to assess how to use money, we need to consider people.

Is it not then time to reinforce the study of philosophy in education? In a market society, where the overwhelming aim is to enhance monetary gain, philosophy is not seen to have an important role. The ability to maximize monetary gain, in terms of future earning power, continues to be a primary objective of education. In a humanistic society that values interpersonal relationships and happiness, philosophy has a vital role. The person must make money in order to live, but must also understand the place of values in human behaviour and how they influence outcome. The person needs to understand love and virtue.

Institutional reform is part of the changing landscape and this has started in the financial world. Although the job is far from done, and lobbying by the financial sector to reverse legislation and render it ineffective persists, government action has begun to enable a more robust financial system, one where there is less abuse. If we are to develop business, economic and financial management theory to provide for a humanistic world, much work lies ahead. Not only must the human being and nature replace money at the centre of society, but human aspirations must be understood and engaged with. Management study cannot rest on abstract theory; it must extend to philosophy and the humanities.

Amoral, Immoral or Ethical?

We currently tend to see business as amoral: the discussion of morality has no place there. We believe that in an extended, and by definition abstract world, morals are not necessary and in fact impractical. The market and profit will substitute for morals, as this is instrumentally perfect and will ensure that the economic pie is shared through the invisible hand. In order for the pie to grow, monetary return must be maximized. Recent history has revealed the fallacy of this position.

Our society takes the fragmentation of the person for granted, thus justifying manipulation and deceit in order to attain ambition. We think it is part of the process of survival and success. For this reason Machiavelli's *The Prince*, much favoured by business consultants, serves as a guide for strategy and wily manipulation, while his *Discourses on Livy* is overlooked. Concurrently, we subscribe to Hobbes's vision of amoral human nature, with law and state ensuring restraint, because humans are motivated by fear not love. In business today, we focus on the law and not behaviour. As long as business activity meets legal requirements, it is acceptable, and loopholes are exploited as legal failings rather than moral failings. But virtue goes beyond adherence to the law. It implies consideration for the outcome of action. To what extent might an action hurt the other while benefitting oneself? We should be guided not only by fear, but also by love.

Reform of our economic, financial and business system to enable it to serve the human being will be a long journey. Unless we bring back humanist considerations, no true remedy to our crisis is possible. In our discussion of the common good, we have seen how a well-functioning institutional framework and good human behaviour complement one another. In the long term, we need an economic, financial and business model that offers material goods with beneficial efficiency and with respect for humans and for nature. Work need not be purely functional; it can permit dignity. A humanist model does not allow for excessive extraction in the form of salary, bonus or profit. It considers proportionality, which Aristotle equates with justice. The market can then be characterized by fairness and reciprocity, where all parties to the exchange benefit and nature is not sacrificed. It can incorporate friendship and virtue.

Investment and profits are indispensable to enable the economic wheel to continue to turn. Investment looks to the present and the future. Beneficial investment has a long-term orientation and includes a response to the environmental challenges we face. The equity market can channel capital into productive enterprises. It need not be an arena for short-term manipulation or a black box to put long-term investors at a disadvantage. Processes are in place to help us with the transition,[13] but meaningful action is yet to come. Such a move can be led by institutional investors, such as pension funds, foundations and country wealth funds.[14] Private individuals within the 1% can also play a vital role. Their response to the challenges the world faces need not simply be through giving some of their wealth to charity, but also by contributing to a sustainable investment paradigm. Visible examples will help to gain traction for meaningful change.

With advances in technology, the financial system will undergo great transformation. Complementary and alternative currencies, even virtual money, are likely to become used more widely. Hyman Minsky writes: "anyone can create money; the problem lies in getting it accepted".[15] Future developments may modify our financial system beyond recognition.[16] Some changes may bring benefit, while others may further compound speculative opportunities, debt build-up or excessive wealth extraction.[17] However, creative and beneficial innovation can make the economy and society more resilient.

Whatever the future for finance, the need for trust remains. Trust is only possible with responsible action, where we refrain from behaviour that might benefit ourselves in the short term but jeopardize society or nature. Some think of such restraint as sacrifice, but it cannot be if we consider our interlinkages with each other and with nature, if we consider ourselves as part of the whole. Seen through a holistic prism, no action detrimental to others and to nature can be beneficial to us. E.F. Schumacher, the first of the holistic economists, recognized the importance of integral thinking, of looking at the impact of one's actions on the whole system.[18] He realized the folly of extracting benefit at the expense of another and of resolving a problem by shifting it to another sphere. A humanistic economic and financial system is essential. It requires love and virtue to work alongside money.

Expanding an Imagined Ideal

Working towards a humanistic society requires constant attention, for divergent paths pull at us. E. F. Schumacher writes that the establishment of an ethical foundation does not call for "new inventions [but] development of man's higher faculties and their application".[19] It is a process of cultivation over time and necessitates deep reflection, an indispensable component of true knowledge. Love and virtue require self-awareness. We recall Thomas Aquinas – influenced by Heraclitus and as recounted by Joseph Pieper – who believed that knowledge is complete only with both *ratio* (reason) and *intellectus* (contemplation). Whereas the advance of science initially took us away from the practice of contemplation or meditation at the dawn of Modernity, science is now bringing us back to it. Neuroscientists assert its importance, validated by research findings. However, we should not need science to tell us of its timeless merit, to remind us of wisdom.

Deep reflection helps us to attain understanding and true knowledge and enables beneficial action to spread. We have seen the power of example in striking the imagination and calling forth mimesis. Goodness, manifest via love and virtue, is contagious. It spreads. Love, the infinite resource, propagates love and provides fertile ground for virtue. It is where transformation lies and a new reality is born, one where we can live in unity and harmony. This is how a humanistic society is born.

Its birth may appear far off. But the historian Norman Davies said: "Historical change is like an avalanche. The starting point is a snow-covered mountainside that looks solid. All the changes take place under the surface and are rather invisible. But something is coming. What is impossible is to say when."[20] Let us hope that what comes will not be disruptive like an avalanche, but nourishing like a river flowing underground before showing itself one day. Human history is dynamic. It is unknown in advance, even if human behaviour influences its course. We are free to choose, and our action determines what is to come.

Is hope for a humanistic society unrealistic? Utopian? The sociologist Anthony Giddens differentiates between utopianism and utopian realism, which he defines as envisaging "alternative futures whose very propagation might help them [to] be realized".[21] We need to base the future on a utopian vision of a more caring world order. There are two kinds of dreams. One is fantasy, an escape from an ugly reality, but it is always slipping away because reality remains in its tedious, overwhelming and alienating form. The other dream, imagination, has the creative power to build something new, dynamic and lasting.

I leave it for you to imagine what the future can hold and to work towards an *imagined ideal* that will serve humanity in a new reality that calls for compassion and collaboration. The response to our crisis lies not in any one solution, but in exploring the right questions, for the solution is found in each of us, living love and virtue in harmony with money, not in discord.

Bibliography

Acemoglu, Daron and James A Robinson (2013) *Why Nations Fail: The Origins of Power, Prosperity and Poverty*, Profile Books

Acharya, Viral V and Philipp Schnabl (2008) 'How Banks Play the Leverage "Game"', *NYU Stern White Papers Project,* http://bit.ly/tpMLV13

Admati, Anat (2013) 'We're all still hostages to the big banks', *New York Times,* Aug. 25, 2013

Admati, Anat and Martin Hellwig (2013) *The Bankers' New Clothes: What's Wrong with Banking and What to Do About It*, Princeton University Press

Akerlof, George A and Robert J Shiller (2009) *Animal Spirits: How Human Psychology Drives the Economy and Why It Matters for Global Capitalism*, Princeton University Press

Albrow, Martin (2009) 'Deconstructing Globalization,', *Books and Ideas*, June 4, 2009

Allen, Kate *et al.* (2014) 'George Osborne facing growing calls to scale back Help to Buy', *Financial Times,* May 7, 2014. http://bit.ly/tpMLV49

Alloway, Tracy and Kara Scannell (2013) 'Jury finds Tourre defrauded investors', *Financial Times,* Aug. 1, 2013. http://bit.ly/tpMLV09

Anderson, Carl (2008) *A Civilization of Love: What Every Catholic Can Do to Transform the World*, Harper One

Anderson, Sarah *et al.* (2010) *Executive Excess 2010: CEO Pay and the Great Recession,* Institute for Policy Studies

Appiah, Kwame Anthony (2008) *Experiments in Ethics,* Harvard University Press

Aquinas, Thomas (1272/1984) *Treatise on the Virtues* (trans. John Oesterle), University of Notre Dame Press

------ (1274/2006) *Summa Theologiae*, http://bit.ly/tpMLV99

Arendt, Hannah (1929/1996) *Love and St. Augustine*, University of Chicago Press

Aristotle, (350 BCE/1908) *Nicomachean Ethics* (trans. W. D. Ross) Internet Classics Archive. http://bit.ly/tpMLV01

------ (350 BCE/1986) *The Politics* (trans. William Ellis), Prometheus Books

Armstrong, Karen (2011) *Twelve Steps to a Compassionate Life*, The Bodley Head

Augustine, (401) *Confessions* (trans. Edward Bouverie Pusey) http://bit.ly/tpMLV101

------ (417) 'On the Holy Trinity' (ed. Philip Schaff) http://bit.ly/tpMLV100

Barber, Tony (2012) 'Lunch with the FT: Norman Davies', *Financial Times*, Oct. 19, 2012 http://bit.ly/tpMLV54

Barker, Alex (2013) 'EU ready to set tough bank pay curbs', *Financial Times*, Feb. 17, 2013 http://bit.ly/tpMLV62

Beinhocker, Eric and Nick Hanauer (2014) 'Redefining Capitalism', *McKinsey Quarterly*, September 2014. http://bit.ly/tpMLV56

Bentham, Jeremy (1789/1907) *An Introduction to the Principles of Morals and Legislation*, Clarendon Press

Blinder, Alan S (2013) *After the Music Stopped: The Financial Crisis, the Response, and the Work Ahead*, Penguin Press

Blyth, Mark (2013) *Austerity: The History of a Dangerous Idea,* Oxford University Press

Bobbitt, Philip (2013) *The Garments of Court and Palace: Machiavelli and the World that He Made*, Atlantic Books

Bok, Sissela (2010) *Exploring Happiness: From Aristotle to Brain Science,* Yale University Press

Boltanski, Luc (1990) *L'Amour et la Justice Comme Compétences*, Éditions Métailié

Bordo, Michael and Andrew Filardo (2005) 'Deflation in a Historical Perspective', BIS Working Paper No. 186, Nov. 2005. http://bit.ly/tpMLV46

Braudel, Fernande (1971) *Afterthoughts on Material Civilization and Capitalism*, John Hopkins University Press

Bronk, Richard (2009) *The Romantic Economist*, Cambridge University Press

Bruni, Luigino (2006) *Civil Happiness: Economics and Human Flourishing in Historical Perspective*, Routledge

------ (2012a) *The Genesis and Ethos of the Market*, Palgrave Macmillan

------ (2012b) *Le Nuove Virtù del Mercato, nell'Era dei Beni Commune*, Città Nuova

Bruni, Luigino and Robert Sugden (2008) 'Fraternity: Why the Market Need Not Be a Morally Free Zone', *Economics and Philosophy,* 24 (2008) 35-64

Bruni, Luigino and Stefano Zamagni (2007) *Civil Economy: Efficiency, Equity, Public Happiness,* Peter Lang

------ (2013) *Handbook on the Economics of Reciprocity and Social Enterprise,* Edward Elgar

Buber, Martin (1965/2002) *The Way of Man*, Routledge

Bullock, Nicole and Philip Stafford (2014) 'Goldman Sachs fined in dark pool debacle', *Financial Times,* July 1, 2014. http://bit.ly/tpMLV24

Carlyle, Thomas (1882) *Last Words on Trade Unions Promoterism and the Sign of the Times*, William Patterson http://bit.ly/tpMLV98

Carney, Mark, (2014) 'Inclusive Capitalism', speech at the Conference on Inclusive Capitalism. http://bit.ly/tpMLV76

Cassidy, John (2014) 'Forces of Divergence', *New Yorker*, March 31, 2014

Chang, Ha-Joon (2014) *Economics: The User's Guide,* Pelican Books

Cheng, François (2009) *The Way of Beauty: Five Meditations for Spiritual Transformation*, Inner Traditions

Coda, Piero (2008) *Sul Luogo della Trinità,* Città Nuova

------ (2010) 'The Experience and Understanding of the Faith in God – Trinity from Saint Augustine to Chiara Lubich', *New Humanity Review Excerpts,* No. 15

Coleridge, Samuel Taylor (1817) 'A Lay Sermon Addressed to the Higher and Middle Classes on the Existing Distresses and Discontents' http://bit.ly/tpMLV97

Crowley, Roger (2011) *City of Fortune: How Venice Won and Lost A Naval Empire*, Faber & Faber

Dalai Lama (2013) *Beyond Religion: Ethics for a Whole World*, Rider

Damasio, Antonio (2010a) *Self Comes to Mind: Constructing the Conscious Brain*, Knopf Doubleday

------ (2010b) Templeton Foundation Big Question: 'Does Moral Action Depend on Reasoning?' http://bit.ly/tpMLV60

Darwin, Charles (1871) *The Descent of Man, and Selection in Relation to Sex*

Davies, Norman (1997) *Europe: A History,* Pimlico

de Waal, F and Stefanie Preston (2002) 'Empathy: ultimate and proximate bases', *Behavioural and Brain Sciences,* Vol. 25, Issue 1, Feb. 2002, pp. 1-20.

Dichter, Ernest (1960) *Strategy of Desire*, Doubleday

Duerksen, Roland A., ed. (1970) *Shelley: Political Writings,* Meredith

Ellul, Jacques (1964) *The Technological Society*, Knopf

Faulks, Sebastian (2009) *A Week in December,* Hutchinson

Ferguson, Niall (2009) *The Ascent of Money: A Financial History of the World*, Penguin

Ferry, Luc (2010) *La Révolution de l'Amour: Pour Une Spiritualité Laique*, Plon

Fisher, Irving (1930) *The Theory of Interest,* Macmillan

Fleming, Sam & Philip Stafford (2014) 'Financial Conduct Authority sets sights on high-frequency traders', *Financial Times*, July 9, 2014. http://bit.ly/tpMLV15

Fontaine, Laurence (2008) *L'Économie Morale: Pauvreté, Credit et Confiance dans l'Europe Préindustrielle*, Gallimard

Foster, John Bellamy and Fred Magdoff (2009) *The Great Financial Crisis: Causes and Consequences*, Monthly Review Press

Fox, Justin (2009) *The Myth of the Rational Market: A History of Risk, Reward, and Delusion on Wall Street*, Harper Collins

Frank, Robert H. and Ben S. Bernanke, 3rd ed. (2007) *Principles of Macro-Economics,* McGraw-Hill

Frankfurt, Henry G. (2004) *The Reasons of Love*, Princeton University Press

Frankl, Victor (1959/2004) *Man's Search for Meaning,* Rider

Fraser, Steve (2005) *Every Man a Speculator: A History of Wall Street in American Life*, Harper Collins

Freud, Sigmund (1920/2003) 'The Ego and the Id' in *Beyond the Pleasure Principle and Other Writings,* Penguin

------ (1934) 'Mourning and Melancholia', *Collected Papers,* Vol. 4. (ed. E. Jones, trans. J. Riviere), The Hogarth Press

Frey, Bruno (2008) *Happiness: A Revolution in Economics*, MIT Press

Friedman, Milton (1953) 'The Methodology of Positive Economics' in *Essays in Positive Economics*, University of Chicago Press

Fuller, Buckminster (1981) *Critical Path*, St Martin's Press

Galbraith, John Kenneth (1975) *Money: Whence It Came, Where It Went,* Penguin Books

Galbraith, John Kenneth and Nicole Salinger (1981) *Almost Everyone's Guide to Economics,* Pelican Books

Geithner, Timothy (2014) *Stress Test: Reflections on Financial Crises,* Random House Business

Georgescu-Roegen, Nicholas (1975), 'Energy and Economic Myths', *Southern Economic Journal,* Vol. 41, Number 3

Giddens, Anthony (1991) *The Consequences of Modernity*, Polity Press

Gilbert, Daniel (2006) *Stumbling on Happiness*, Knopf

Giles, Chris and Sarah O'Connor (2014) 'Haldane backs central banks' action in a "nutty" world', *Financial Times,* July 2, 2014. http://bit.ly/tpMLV52

Gore, Al (2013) *The Future*, WH Allen

Habermas, Jürgen (1989) *The Structural Transformation of the Public Sphere: An Inquiry into a Category of Bourgeois Society*, Polity Press

Hanh, Thich Nhat (1993) *Love in Action*, Parallax Press

------ (2003) *The Art of Power*, Harper One

Hardin, Garrett, 'The Tragedy of the Commons', *Science,* Vol. 162, Dec. 13, 1968, pp. 1243-1248

Hawking, Stephen and Leonard Mlodinow (2010) *The Grand Design,* Bantam Books

Hayek, Friedrich (1931) *Prices and Production,* George Routledge & Sons

------ (1945) 'The Use of Knowledge in Society', *The American Economic Review*, Vol. 35, no. 4, Sept. 1945, pp. 522-528

Herndon, Thomas, Michael Ash and Robert Pollin (2013) 'Does High Public Debt Consistently Stifle Economic Growth? A Critique of Reinhart and Rogoff', Political Economy Research Institute Working Paper Series No. 322, April 15, 2013. http://bit.ly/tpMLV66

Hirschman, Albert O. (1977/1997) *The Passions and the Interests: Political Arguments for Capitalism before its Triumph*, Princeton University Press

Hitchens, Christopher (2005) *Love, Poverty and War: Journeys and Essays,* Atlantic Books

Ho, Karen (2009) *Liquidated: An Ethnography of Wall Street*, Duke University Press

Hobbes, Thomas (1642/1651/2000) *De Cive,* Blackmask Online, http://bit.ly/tpMLV51

------ (1651/1997) *Leviathan, or the Matter, Forme and Power of A Common-Wealth Ecclesiasticall and Civill*, W.W. Norton

Hoffman, Martin (2000) *Empathy and Moral Development*, Cambridge University Press

Horkheimer, Max (1946) *Eclipse of Reason*, Continuum

Ingham, Geoffrey K (2004) *The Nature of Money,* Polity

Isaacson, Walter (2011) *Steve Jobs,* Simon & Schuster

Jackendoff, Ray (2007) *Language, Consciousness, Culture: Essays on Mental Structure*, MIT Press

Jenkins, Patrick (2013) 'Vickers calls for doubling bank capital levels', *Financial Times,* Sept. 9, 2013. http://bit.ly/tpMLV19

Jones, Claire and Sam Fleming (2014) 'BIS urges central banks to exit loose monetary policy', *Financial Times,* June 29, 2014. http://bit.ly/tpMLV42

Jones, Daniel Stedman (2012) *Masters of the Universe: Hayek, Friedman, and the Birth of Neoliberal Politics*, Princeton University Press

Kahneman, Daniel (2011) *Thinking Fast and Slow,* Farrar, Straus and Giroux

Kaplan, David A. (2012) 'Hostess is bankrupt… again', *Fortune,* Aug. 13, 2012

Kay, John (2009) 'Future of investing', *Financial Times,* Oct. 2, 2009. http://bit.ly/tpMLV10

------ (2014) '"Trust me, I am a financial advisor" is not good enough', *Financial Times,* Jan. 27, 2015. http://bit.ly/tpMLV35

------ (2015) 'History is antidote to fear of falling prices', *Financial Times,* July 8, 2014. http://bit.ly/tpMLV109

Keynes, John Maynard (1930a) *A Treatise on Money*, Vol. II, Macmillan

------ (1930b) 'Economic Possibilities for our Grandchildren' in *Essays in Persuasion, The Collected Writings of John Maynard Keynes* (1931) Macmillan

------ (1936) *The General Theory of Employment, Interest, and Money*, Macmillan

Kindleberger, Charles P. and Robert Z. Aliber (2011) *Manias, Panics and Crashes. A History of Financial Crises,* Palgrave MacMillan

King, Martin Luther Jr. (1967) 'Beyond Vietnam: A Time to Break Silence', Speech at Riverside Church, New York City April 4, 1967. http://bit.ly/tpMLV59

Kirk, G.S., J.E. Raven and M. Schofield (1983) *The Presocratic Philosophers*, Cambridge University Press

Klein, Naomi (2014) *This Changes Everything: Capitalism vs. the Climate,* Allen Lane,

Kozel, Philip (2006) *Market Sense: Toward A New Economics of Markets and Society*, Routledge

Krishnamurti, 'The Last Talks', Madras, December 1985. http://bit.ly/tpMLV03

Kristeva, Julia (2011) 'Some Principles for the Humanism of the 21st Century', Assisi, Oct. 27, 2011. http://bit.ly/tpMLV02

Kumar, Satish (2012) 'Money and Morality', *Resurgence*, Issue 270, Jan./Feb., 2012. http://bit.ly/tpMLV80

Lanier, Jaron (2010) *You Are Not A Gadget: A Manifesto*, Alfred A Knopf

Layard, Richard (2005) *Happiness: Letters from a New Science*, Penguin Books

Lewin, Shira (1996) 'Economics & Psychology: Lessons for Our Own Day from the Early 20th Century', *Journal of Economic Literature,* Vol. 34, Issue 3, Sept. 1996, 1293.1323

Lewis, C.S. (1966) *A Grief Observed,* Faber & Faber

------ (1988) *The Four Loves*, Harcourt Brace

Lewis, Michael (2011) *The Big Short: Inside the Doomsday Machine*, W.W. Norton

------ (2014a) 'The Wolf Hunters of Wall Street', *New York Times,* Mar. 31, 2014

------ (2014b) *Flash Boys: Cracking the Money Code*, Allen Lane

Locke, John (1690/1970) *Two Treatises of Government,* Cambridge University Press

Lowenstein, Roger (2000) *When Genius Failed: The Rise and Fall of Long-Term Capital Management*, Random House

Machiavelli, Niccolò (1517/1531/1997) *Discourses on Livy*, Oxford University Press, trans. Julia and Peter Bondanella

------ (1532/1999) *The Prince*, Penguin Books

MacIntyre, Alaisdair (2006) *Ethics and Politics: Selected Essays,* Cambridge University Press

Mandeville, Bernard (1714/1924) *The Fable of the Bees,* Clarendon Press

Marion, Jean-Luc (2003) *The Erotic Phenomenon*, University of Chicago Press

Maritain, Jacques (1946/1967) *The Person and the Common Good*, University of Notre Dame Press

Martin, Michelle (2012) 'Q+A - What is shadow banking and why does it matter?', Reuters, Feb. 7, 2012. http://bit.ly/tpMLV16

Melo Antunes, Maria (2007) 'Will Principles of Sustainability be Increasingly Incorporated in Mainstream Equity Investment?' Unpublished MSc thesis, Imperial College London

Mian, Atif and Amir Sufi (2014) *House of Debt: How They (and You) Caused the Great Recession and How We Can Prevent it from Happening Again*, University of Chicago Press

Mill, John Stuart (1848) *The Principles of Political Economy*, Longmans, Green

------ (1859/1869/2006) *On Liberty and The Subjection of Women*, Penguin Classics

------ (1865/1908) *Auguste Comte and Positivism*, George Routledge & Sons

------ (1868/2001) *Utilitarianism*, Hackett Publishing

------ (2006) *Collected Works of John Stuart Mill: Autobiography and Literary Essays*, Liberty Fund

Minsky, Hyman P, (1978) 'The Financial Instability Hypothesis: A Restatement', Thames Papers in Political Economy, Thames Polytechnic

------ (2008) *Stabilizing an Unstable Economy*, McGraw Hill

Mises, Ludwig von (1953) *The Theory of Money and Credit,* Yale University Press

Montaigne, Michel de (1991) *The Complete Essays,* Penguin Books

Morgenson, Gretche (2015) 'New Congress already taking aim at Dodd-Frank', *International NY Times,* Jan. 12, 2015

Nieli, Russell (2006) 'Critic of the Sensate Culture: Rediscovering the Genius of Pitirim Sorokin', *The Political Science Reviewer* (Intercollegiate Studies Institute) 35: 264-379.

Nussbaum, Martha C. (2001a) *The Fragility of Goodness: Luck and Ethics in Greek Tragedy and Philosophy*, Cambridge University Press

------ (2001b) *Upheavals of Thought: The Intelligence of Emotions*, Cambridge University Press

------ (2013a) *Political Emotions: Why Love Matters for Justice*, Harvard University Press

------ (2013b) 'Understanding Empathy: Philosophical, Neuroscientific and Psychological Approaches', Interview on 21st Century Enlightenment by Matthew Taylor, RSA http://bit.ly/tpMLV58

O'Connor, Sarah, Emily Cadman and Sharlene Goff (2014) 'Lagarde and Carney let fire at financial sector', *Financial Times,* May 27, 2014. http://bit.ly/tpMLV32

O'Neill, Onora (2002) 'A Question of Trust', BBC Radio 4 Reith Lectures

Pacioli, Luca (1494) *Review of Arithmetic, Geometry, Ratio and Proportion*

Packard, Jim and Elizabeth Rigby (2011) 'Cameron backs archbishop on bankers', *Financial Times,* Nov. 2, 2011. http://bit.ly/tpMLV50

Phillipson, Nicholas (2010) *Adam Smith: An Enlightened Life*, Allen Lane

Pieper, Josef (1947) *Leisure: the Basis of Culture*, Faber & Faber

Piketty, Thomas (2014) *Capital in the Twenty-First Century,* Harvard University Press

Pope Benedict XVI (2009) Third Encyclical: *Charity in Truth*

Pope Francis (2013) Apostolic Exhortation: *Evangelii Gaudium*

Putnam, Hilary (2004) *Ethics without Ontology*, Harvard University Press

Putnam, Robert (2000) *Bowling Alone: The Collapse and Revival of American Community*, Simon & Schuster

Rachmeon, Gideon (2014) 'Growth and globalization can't cure all the world's ill', *Financial Times,* Jan. 28, 2014. http://bit.ly/tpMLV11

Raghuram, Rajan (2013) 'The Paranoid Style in Economics', Project Syndicate, Aug. 17, 2013. http://bit.ly/tpMLV70

Rand, Ayn (1964) *The Virtue of Selfishness,* Signet

Reinhart, Carmen M and Kenneth S. Rogoff (2009) *This Time is Different: Eight Centuries of Financial Folly,* Princeton University Press

------ (2010) 'Growth in A Time of Debt', National Bureau of Economic Research Working Paper 15639 http://bit.ly/tpMLV65

Ricoeur, Paul (1992) *Oneself as Another,* University of Chicago Press

Rifkin, Jeremy (2010) *The Empathic Civilization: The Race to Global Consciousness in a World of Crisis*, Polity Press

------ (2014) *The Zero Marginal Cost Society,* Palgrave Macmillan

Rizzolatti, G and Laila Craighero (2004) 'The Mirror-Neuron System', *Annual Review of Neuroscience* 2004. 27:169-92. http://bit.ly/tpMLV36

Robertson, Dennis H (1954) 'What does the Economist Economize?' reprinted in his *Economic Commentaries,* 1956, Staples Press, pp. 147-154

Ruskin, John (1862/2010) *Unto This Last,* Pallas Athene

Sandel, Michael J. (2010) *Justice: What's the Right Thing to Do?,* Macmillan

------ (2012) *What Money Can't Buy: The Moral Limits of Markets*, Farrar, Straus and Giroux

Sandor, Richard (2012) *Good Derivatives: A Story of Financial and Environmental Innovation*, John Wiley

Sartre, Jean-Paul (1946) 'Existentialism is a Humanism', in Kaufman, Walter, ed. (1956/89) *Existentialism from Dostoyevsky to Sartre,* Meridian Publishing

Scannell, Kara, 'Former Madoff lieutenants on trial', *Financial Times,* Oct. 6, 2013. http://bit.ly/tpMLV21

------ (2014) 'SEC: With the Program', *Financial Times,* May 9, 2014. http://bit.ly/tpMLV20

Scannell, Kara and Nicole Bullock (2014) 'Top NY securities regulator sues Barclays over "dark pool"', *Financial Times,* June 26, 2014. http://bit.ly/tpMLV23

Schafer, Daniel (2014) 'EU banks beat bonus caps with cash allowances', *Financial Times*, July 20, 2014. http://bit.ly/tpMLV63

Schibli, Hermann S. (1990) *Pherekydes of Syros*, Clarendon Press

Schopenhauer, Arthur (1840/1995) *On the Basis of Morality*, Berghahn Books

Schumacher, E. F. (1973) *Small Is Beautiful: A Study of Economics As If People Mattered*, Vintage Books

------ (1977) *A Guide for the Perplexed*, Vintage Books

Schumpeter, Joseph A. (1934/1983) *The Theory of Economic Development: An Inquiry into Profits, Capital, Credit, Interest, and the Business Cycle*, Transaction Books

Screpanti, Ernesto & Stefano Zamagni (2005) *An Outline of the History of Economic Thought*, Oxford University Press

Scruton, Roger (2000) *Modern Culture*, St Augustine's Press

Sen, Amartya (2010) *The Idea of Justice,* Belknap Press

Sheridan, Barrett (2008) 'The $600 Trillion Derivatives Market', *Newsweek,* Oct. 18, 2008. http://bit.ly/tpMLV17

Shiller, Robert J. (2000) *Irrational Exuberance*, Princeton University Press

------ (2012) *Finance and the Good Society*, Princeton University Press

Shotter, James and Alex Barker (2013) 'Swiss Vote for Corporate Pay Curbs', *Financial Times,* March 3, 2013. http://bit.ly/tpMLV75

Sigmund, Paul E. ed. (1988) *St. Thomas Aquinas on Politics and Ethics,* W.W. Norton

Skidelsky, Robert and Edward Skidelsky (2012) *How Much is Enough? The Love of Money and the Case for the Good Life*, Allen Lane

Skinner, Quentin (1981) *Machiavelli: A Very Short Introduction*, Oxford University Press

Skousen, Mark (2007) *The Big Three in Economics*, ME Sharpe

Smith, Adam (1759/1976) *The Theory of Moral Sentiments*, Oxford University Press

------ (1776/1998) *The Wealth of Nations,* Oxford University Press

Smith, Greg (2012) *Why I Left Goldman Sachs: A Wall Street Story*, Grand Central Publishing

Sorokin, Pitirim A. (1954/1982) *The Ways and Power of Love: Types. Factors and Techniques of Moral Transformation*, Templeton Foundation Press

Steinbeck, John (1939/1988) *The Grapes of Wrath,* Octopus Books

Stiglitz, Joseph (2003) *The Roaring Nineties: Seeds of Destruction*, W.W. Norton

------ (2012) *The Price of Inequality*, Allen Lane

Stiglitz, Joseph, Amartya Sen and Jean-Paul Fitoussi (2009) 'Report by the Commission on the Measurement of Economic Performance and Social Progress'. http://bit.ly/tpMLV83

Tagore, Rabindranath (1928) 'The Voice of Humanity' in *Lectures and Addresses*, Macmillan

Teilhard de Chardin, Pierre (1959/2004) *The Future of Man*, Doubleday

------ (1959/2002) *The Phenomenon of Man*, Perennial

Tett, Gillian (2009) *Fool's Gold: How Unrestrained Greed Corrupted A Dream, Shattered Global Markets and Unleashed A Catastrophe*, Little, Brown

------ (2013a) 'An Interview with Alan Greenspan', Oct. 25, 2013. http://bit.ly/tpMLV33

------ (2013b) 'West's debt explosion is real story behind Fed QE dance', *Financial Times*, Sept. 19, 2013. http://bit.ly/tpMLV48

Thompson, Nicholas (2014) 'Who shared the electric car?' *New Yorker,* June 13, 2014. http://bit.ly/tpMLV12

Tillich, Paul (1960) *Love, Power and Justice: Ontological Analyses and Ethical Applications*, Oxford University Press

Tobin, James (1984) 'On the Efficiency of the Financial System', Fred Hirsch Memorial Lecture, published in *Lloyd's Bank Review*, No. 153, July 1984, pp. 1-15

Turkle, Sherry (2011) *Alone Together: Why We Expect More from Technology and Less from Each Other*, Basic Books

Turner, Adair (2010) 'Economics, conventional wisdom and public policy', presented at the Institute for New Economic Thinking Inaugural Conference, Cambridge, Apr. 8, 2010. http://bit.ly/tpMLV34

------ (2013a) 'Credit, Money and Leverage: What Wicksell, Hayek and Fisher Knew and Modern Macroeconomics Forgot', Stockholm School of Economics, Sept. 12, 2013. http://bit.ly/tpMLV71

------ (2013b) 'Debt, Money and Mephistopheles', Feb 6, 2013, Cass Business School. http://bit.ly/tpMLV73

------ (2014) 'Creating money, for what purpose?' Presentation at the LSE, March 21, 2014, http://bit.ly/tpMLV68

Varela, Francisco (1999) *Ethical Know-How: Action, Wisdom and Cognition,* Stanford University Press

Veblen, Thorstein (1899/2007) *The Theory of the Leisure Class*, Oxford University Press

------ (1932) *The Place of Science in Modern Civilization*, Viking Press

Washingtonsblog (2012) 'Top Derivatives Expert Estimates Size of the Global Derivatives Market at $1,200 Trillion Dollars', May 18, 2012. http://bit.ly/tpMLV18

Waters, Richard (2014) 'Silicon Valley's rush to back Bitcoin services rouses concern', *Financial Times*, May 27, 2014. http://bit.ly/tpMLV57

Wessel, David (2009) *In Fed We Trust: Ben Bernanke's War on the Great Panic*, Crown

White, William (2012) 'Ultra Easy Monetary Policy and the Law of Unintended Consequences', Federal Reserve Bank of Dallas Working Paper No. 126. http://bit.ly/tpMLV53

Wilber, Ken (2000) *Grace and Grit,* Shambhala

Wilkinson, Richard and Kate Pickett (2010) *The Spirit Level: Why Equality is Better for Everyone*, Penguin Books

------ (2014) 'How Inequality hollows out the soul', *New York Times*, Feb. 2, 2014 http://bit.ly/tpMLV81

Williams, Rowan (2011) 'Time for us to challenge the idols of high finance', *Financial Times*, Nov. 1, 2011 http://bit.ly/tpMLV61

Wilson, Edward O. (2012) *The Social Conquest of the Earth,* Liveright Publishing

Wolf, Martin (2013a) '"Too big to fail" is too big to ignore', *Financial Times,* April 15, 2014. http://bit.ly/tpMLV45

------ (2013b) 'The Case for Helicopter Money', *Financial Times*, Feb. 13, 2013 http://bit.ly/tpMLV74

------ (2014a) 'Disarm our doomsday machine', *Financial Times,* May 27, 2014, http://bit.ly/tpMLV14

------ (2014b) 'Bad advice from Basel's Jeremiah', *Financial Times*, July 1, 2014. http://bit.ly/tpMLV69

------ (2014c) *The Shifts and the Shocks: What We've Learned – and Have Still to Learn – from the Financial Crisis*, Allen Lane

Woolley, Paul (2013) 'Momentum investing is bad for your wealth', *Financial Times*, July 12, 2013. http://bit.ly/tpMLV55

Wooley, Paul and Dimitri Vayanos (2012) 'Taming the Finance Monster', *Central Banking Journal,* Dec. 2012 http://bit.ly/tpMLV44

Yellen, Janet (2014) 'Monetary Policy and Financial Stability', Federal Reserve Board speech, June 29, 2014. http://bit.ly/tpMLV67

Yunus, Muhammad (1999) *Banker to the Poor: Micro-Lending and the Battle Against World Poverty*, Perseus Books

Zamagni, Stefano, ed. (1995) *The Economics of Altruism,* Edward Elgar

------(2011) "Globalização e o Pensamento Econômico Franciscano," *Cadernos IHU Ideias*, Ano 9, N° 153, 2011

Notes

Introduction

[1] Long-Term Capital Management, a hedge fund, was founded in 1994 by John Merriweather, the bond arbitrage star from Salomon Brothers, who had expanded the involvement of mathematicians in financial trading and contributed to the bonus system for traders on Wall Street. It also included among its founding partners Robert C. Merton and Myron Scholes, jointly awarded the Nobel Prize in Economics (1997) for their work related to the pricing of derivatives, thus permitting the development of this market. Until its collapse, the Fund had been providing very high double-digit returns, with no losing stretches, hardly any volatility and seemingly no risk. LTCM used complex mathematical yield curve and option pricing models to take advantage via arbitrage of changes and pricing discrepancies in the yield curve of fixed income instruments and in the volatility of traded securities, on the premise that eventually yield differentials and volatilities would converge to 'fair value'. However, with the Russian debt crisis in 1998 following on the Asian debt crisis the previous year, all markets plunged and volatilities hit unprecedented highs, leaving the fund, with thousands of derivative contracts endlessly intertwined with other banks on Wall Street, helplessly exposed and potentially failing while dragging down other institutions with it, thus requiring intervention by the Fed. See Lowenstein (2000) and Ferguson (2009).

[2] Adam Smith's concept of *self-interest* is used to defend liberal markets. I discuss the inadequacy of this perception of Smith's economic vision later. See Smith (1776/1998).

[3] Fortunately, economists are increasingly venturing back into philosophy and books on this have begun to appear – e.g. Skidelsky & Skidelsky (2012).

[4] Pieper (1947: 33)

[5] See Aquinas, *Quaestiones disputatae de veritate*, quoted in Pieper (1947: 33-34).

[6] Alternative units of exchange are increasingly being explored, to replace our current monetary system. Nonetheless, these units are designed to provide for our material welfare; whatever name they are known by, they serve the purpose of what is called money here.

[7] Lewis (1988: 57)

[8] Aristotle (350/1908)

[9] Aristotle (350/1986: 202)

[10] Margaret Thatcher is reputed to have said that "there is no such thing as society". She may have wanted to emphasize individual effort, which is indeed important, but the general interpretation is that everyone should simply look after his own benefit, in line with the misinterpretation of Adam Smith's *self-interest*. This vision has contributed to the degradation of social ties and economic developments over the last thirty years.

[11] In a speech in Lisbon, the writer and Nobel laureate Mario Vargas Llosa highlighted the dangers that lie in the acceptance and toleration of corruption by society and warned that this can eventually undermine democracy, with government increasingly held hostage by private interests. See *O Público*, July 22, 2014.

[12] Kristeva (2011) and Krishnamurti (1985)

Chapter 1

[1] For more on the topics discussed in these paragraphs, see Aristotle (350/1986) pp. 3, 14, 19, 6, 4, 130, 145-187.

[2] Aristotle (350/1986: 91): "justice, for instance, is a virtue, and so necessary to society, that all others must yield her the precedence".

[3] Aristotle (350/1908: 202)

[4] Kozel (2006)

[5] References in this paragraph are to Aristotle (350/1986: 33 and 147-157).

[6] Aquinas (1274/2006: Qy. 77, Art. 4) quoted by Kozel (2006)

[7] Bruni & Sugden (2008: 43-57)

[8] In Chapter 2 we see evidence of asymmetry in financial transactions today.

[9] Ingham (2004: 3)

[10] Braudel (1971: 9)

[11] Galbraith (1975: 15)

[12] Bruni (2012b: 62)

[13] Keynes (1930a: 217)

[14] Hayek (1931)

[15] Mises (1953). The book was first published in German in 1912.

[16] Keynes (1930a: 217)

[17] The process of financialization is discussed in Chapter 2.

[18] Fontaine (2008: 17) refers to Émile Benveniste's study of the origin of the word.

[19] See Investopedia, http://bit.ly/tpMLV04

[20] A letter of credit is a letter from a bank or guarantor guaranteeing to the seller that a buyer's full payment will be made and on time. See Investopedia, http://bit.ly/tpMLV05.

[21] Acemoglu & Robinson (2013: 152)

[22] Crowley (2011: 279)

[23] Zamagni (2011: 5)

[24] Fontaine (2008: 25)

[25] Aristotle also condemns usury, but in his case this is what he calls "money-making" from trade where "men gain from each other". He described usury as "money bred of money," in Aristotle (350/1986: 19).

[26] Discussion with Prof. Stefano Zamagni, University of Bologna.

[27] Yunus (1999)

[28] Aquinas (1274/2006: Qy. 78). The *commenda* is also mentioned in the discussion above about Venice.

[29] Skousen (2007)

[30] A discussion of the history of money and banking can be found in Galbraith (1975) and in Ferguson (2009).

[31] 'Money creation in the modern economy', *Bank of England Quarterly Bulletin*, 2014 Q1. http://bit.ly/tpMLV38

[32] The article shows that bank deposits make up 97% of money as of December 2013 in the UK.

[33] It was the banking system's failure in managing risk that led to the financial crisis of 2007-08.

[34] QE1 was formally launched in the USA in Dec. 2008. In Nov. 2010, QE2 was introduced, followed by QE3. A tapering program was announced in Dec. 2013 and the QE program was eventually suspended in 2014. This resulted in an expansion of the Fed's balance sheet to $4.5 trillion. In the UK, QE, in force from 2009 through 2012, resulted in an increase in the balance sheet by £375 billion. On January 22, 2015, the European Central Bank finally announced a QE program from March 2015 until September 2016. With expansion at €600 billion a month, the program is planned to total €1.1 trillion. See 'What is quantitative easing?' *The Guardian*, Jan. 22, 2015 http://bit.ly/tpMLV89

[35] Galbraith (1975) and Fraser (2005)

[36] Frank & Bernanke (2007: 284)

[37] For a study of speculative financial bubbles, see for example Kindleberger & Aliber (2011).

[38] Locke (1690/1970)

[39] Hobbes (1651/1997: 115)

[40] Locke (1690/1970: 68)

[41] Braudel (1971)

[42] Hirschman (1977/1997: 52)

[43] For more on the topics discussed in this paragraph, see Smith (1776/1998: 26-27 and 456).

[44] Kozel (2006: 41)

[45] Smith (1759/1976: Part VI, 237-262)

[46] Skousen (2007: 18)

[47] Stiglitz (2012)

[48] Phillipson (2010)

[49] For discussion of capital, see Smith (1776/1998: 166 and 178)

[50] Keynes (1930a: 217)

[51] Skousen (2007: 49)

[52] See Bordo & Filardo (2005) and Kay (2015).

[53] Keynes (1936: 103)

[54] This is equally true today. The focus on the short term renders the investment terrain for serious long-term investors difficult to navigate and often treacherous. And it leads many to believe that, in a world of ST trading and speculation, they will be left behind, through opportunity loss, if they do not participate.

[55] Keynes (1930b: 358-373)

[56] See also the treatment of Keynes's prophecy in Skidelsky & Skidelsky (2012) Chapter 1.

Chapter 2

[1] 'Financialization' is a term used by economists to describe the growing scale and profitability of the financial sector, relative to the 'real' economy.

A good treatment of the process can be found in Foster & Magdoff (2009).

[2] The federal funds rate peaked at 22% in 1981, and the yield on long-term (30-year) bonds reached 15%, a record high. In comparison, the yield at Dec. 18, 2014 was 2.815%. See Bloomberg http://bit.ly/tpMLV47

[3] This freed lending at Savings and Loans Associations and Mutual Savings Banks, eventually leading to the S&L crisis.

[4] This move allowed bank holding companies to own other financial companies. The resulting universal bank holding companies were able to lend affiliates money for trading and investment, jeopardizing the security of depositors. With the major financial crisis in 2008, banks were exposed as having extremely high leverage (of forty times in some cases) and insufficient capital reserves to bear incurred risks. See Acharya & Schnabl (2008).

[5] This allowed the derivatives market to expand exponentially. By 2008, the derivatives market was estimated to have quadrupled in size in six years to $600 trillion; today it remains high and estimates range from $600-$1,200 trillion, or twenty times world GDP, based on the latter figure. See Washingtonsblog (2012). This represents extensive speculative activity, overshadowing *bona fide* hedging for risk protection, and the wide range in market estimates is worrisome, for it hints at inadequate supervision and control. Measurement of the derivatives market is hard to fathom; the figure represents 'notional value' and the real money that exchanges hands is a fraction of this. The notional value is the total value of the assets which the derivative contract covers; hence, the money normally at risk on the part of the investor is but a part of the notional value. See Investopedia, http://bit.ly/tpMLV07

[6] These principles include business conduct and governance, risk management and legal protection. See also WMBA Americas, 'Principles for Enhancing the Safety and Soundness of the Wholesale, Over-the-Counter Markets' at http://bit.ly/tpMLV08

[7] Foster, Bellamy, and Magdof (2009: 54)

[8] 'US Economic Indicators: Corporate Profits in GDP', Yardeni Research Inc., Dec. 23, 2014. http://bit.ly/tpMLV39

[9] Schumpeter (1934/1983). See also treatment of Schumpeter by Luigino Bruni in (2012a) Chapter 2

[10] New technology can require little capital and pay immense returns, as shown in the case of WhatsApp and Instagram.

[11] The story of Steve Jobs is a good illustration. His motivation was to introduce innovative and well designed products for which he envisaged

a use; profits followed because the products proved useful and were well received. See Isaacson (2011). Elon Musk, CEO of Tesla, is another example. In his objective to fast-track adoption of electric vehicles, he opened up all the company's patents, an unprecedented move. See Thompson (2014).

[12] The whole issue of economic growth and globalization is understood today as being complex and not necessarily beneficial in all instances. For example, it has contributed to wage stagnation and rising inequality in the West. See Rachmeon (2014).

[13] Jones (2012: Chapter 6 & Conclusion)

[14] Turner (2010).

[15] Tax-beneficial 401-k and IRA retirement savings plans in the USA, SICAVs in Europe, and similar defined contribution plans in Asia and Latin America. Chile was one of the first countries to encourage private pension investment, through liberal policy advised by Milton Friedman and implemented by his students from the University of Chicago.

[16] For illustration, see Kaplan (2012).

[17] His 1999 speech to the Futures Industry Association is quoted in Fox (2009: xii)

[18] See, for example, Tett (2009).

[19] As illustration, average trading in the foreign exchange market increased from $18 billion per day in 1977 to $1 trillion in 1992 to $2.1 trillion in 2011. It is approximately $5.3 trillion today, as reported in the 'Triennial Central Bank Survey' of the Bank of International Settlements, Sept. 2013 http://bit.ly/tpMLV40. By comparison, global GDP was $75 trillion in 2013. See 'The World Bank: GDP' http://bit.ly/tpMLV41. Granted the foreign exchange figure may include double-counting but, nonetheless, a large part is caused by positions to benefit from currency direction, rather than a real need for commercial exchange. It is important to note that not all foreign exchange transactions are virtual and speculative; in today's world, global trade necessitates vast foreign exchange flows, but speculative positions appear perhaps to dwarf legitimate flows. Our challenge is to distinguish the genuine from the speculative in foreign exchange, commodity and other investments, and the risk this entails. At what point does such speculation become dangerous and destructive? Also see Ferguson (2009: Chapter 6) on the development of 'hot money' or financial speculation.

[20] For a description of the development of the derivative market, see Sandor (2012).

[21] See Introduction, note 1 on LTCM.

[22] Jones & Fleming (2014).

[23] Lewis (2011).

[24] In some cases, these instruments remained in the banks' possession through special investment vehicles within *shadow banking*. An unregulated sector and estimated at 25-30% of the financial industry's activity, it provides credit and liquidity, such as to the mortgage market. Without recourse to Central Bank funding or deposits, it depends on short-term funding, such as asset-backed commercial paper and the repo market, thus making it highly vulnerable to a sudden withdrawal of liquidity, as in 2008. Although shadow banking declined following the financial crisis, it is now back to pre-crisis levels. See Martin (2012). However, some argue that shadow banking is taking on a different role since the crisis and includes financial innovation which can be beneficial. See 'The lure of shadow banking', *The Economist*, May 10, 2014.

[25] See 'Brussels agrees crackdown on credit rating agencies', Trader Instinct, Bank of America Merrill Lynch, Jan. 17, 2013. http://bit.ly/tpMLV43

[26] A credit default swap allows for the buyer of a default protection to receive payment from the underwriter of the guarantee, in the event of default. Compensation for default protection is made via a series of payments (the CDS fee or spread) over the life of the debt instrument. 'Naked' CDS allows for purchase by a speculator of such 'insurance' even without owning the underlying debt security. Invented by JP Morgan in 1994, it increased in use after 2003 and by the end of 2007 was estimated at $62.2 trillion by the International Swaps and Derivatives Association.

[27] As described earlier, the market reached $600 trillion, equivalent to twelve times the size of the world economy, at the height of the credit bubble in 2008. See Sheridan (2008). This activity does not appear to have subsided.

[28] See, for example, the case of Fabrice Tourre of Goldman Sachs, charged by the SEC and indicted of defrauding investors in the case of Abacus 2007-AC1, where clients were led to invest in a fund holding specific mortgages, referenced in 'the synthetic collaterized debt obligation' that hedge fund Paulson & Co. selected for subsequent shorting. See Alloway & Scannell (2013).

[29] Kay (2009)

[30] 'Citigroup chief stays bullish on buy-outs', *Financial Times*, July 9, 2014. http://bit.ly/tpMLV79

[31] Milton Friedman in 1950 memo defending free currency markets, quoted in Fox (2009: 93).

[32] Timothy Geithner acknowledged that bankers were "collateral beneficiaries" of the government's bail-out of banks, in order to prevent a financial calamity from crushing the economy. See Geithner (2014: 502-509) and Edward Luce's book review in the *Financial Times* - http://bit.ly/tpMLV22

[33] Hayek (1945)

[34] See, for example, Lewis (2014b)

[35] Shiller (2012: 179)

[36] Shiller (2000: 60)

[37] Minsky (1978: 14-21)

[38] We saw this in the Bernie Madoff case. See Scannell (2013).

[39] Government has stood ready for this purpose in recent years, in order to defer panic and avoid a cascading financial collapse. Martin Wolf (2014a) refers to Timothy Geithner's (2014) defence of government intervention.

[40] Lewis (2014b: 218) describes the widest travel time increment at two milliseconds. In comparison, he notes that it takes 100 milliseconds to blink quickly. The fastest any high-speed trader's signal could travel from the first exchange it reached to the last one was 350 microseconds, or about one 200th of the time it takes to blink.

[41] See Lewis (2014a). He estimates the loss through the price of shares traded at $160 million per day (applied to an average daily volume in the US stock market of $225 billion).

[42] The FCA is launching a review into competition in the wholesale securities market and to what extent co-location is justified as innovation in HFT. See Fleming & Stafford (2014).

[43] Lewis (2014b: 42)

[44] In March, 2014, the New York State Attorney General announced an investigation of the stock exchanges and the 'dark pools' and their relationships with high-frequency traders. In order to police Wall Street, the SEC has invested in high tech tools to keep pace with traders; see Scannell (2014).

[45] On June 26, 2014, the New York State Attorney General sued Barclays for allegedly favouring high-speed traders using its 'dark pool' trading venue while misleading institutional investors; see Scannell & Bullock (2014). And Goldman Sachs was fined $800,000 for failing to ensure that clients trading met US laws to ensure protection of the investor's right to best price practice; see Bullock & Stafford (2014).

[46] See treatment in Smith (2012).

[47] See treatment in Ho (2009).

[48] Faulks (2009: 102-103)

[49] Anderson *et al.* (2010) quoted by Skidelsky & Skidelsky (2012: 30).

[50] Justin Fox (2009: 280) says that until the mid-1960s the average holding period in a professionally managed portfolio was 7 years; by the late 1990s, it was less than a year, and annual portfolio turnover exceeded 100%. James Tobin (1984) writes that stock turnover in the USA was 60% and the average holding period 19 months.

[51] Shiller (2000: xiv)

[52] President Obama called it "the defining challenge of our time". See White House Press Release, Dec. 4, 2013. http://bit.ly/tpMLV25 . Pope Francis (2013: §53) denounced an economy of exclusion and inequality as "an economy that kills" and to the World Economic Forum at Davos in 2014, he termed it a "global risk". See *Global Risks 2014*: Ninth Edition. http://bit.ly/tpMLV26. In Chapter 3, we discuss inequality further.

[53] Piketty (2014) defines as capital any asset that generates a return, encompassing physical capital, such as real estate and factories; intangibles such as brands and patents; and financial assets, such as stocks and bonds. In our times, financial assets and real estate have played a major role.

[54] Piketty uses tax data (since the end of the 18th century for France, the start of the 20th century for the USA and the UK, and more recently for other countries) to argue his case. His work is backed by research by Emmanuel Saez of UC Berkeley and Anthony Atkinson of Oxford. These researchers have provided much of the data we now use to look at inequality and created the World Top Incomes Database, covering thirty countries. Piketty's calculations were questioned subsequently by Chris Giles, Economics Editor of the *Financial Times* on May 23, 2014 http://bit.ly/tpMLV27. See also Piketty's response at http://bit.ly/tpMLV28. Most agree that, despite this contention, Piketty's analysis still holds – see 'Picking holes in Piketty', *The Economist*, May 31, 2014, p. 66

[55] See 'The Rich are Different,' *The Economist*, March 19, 2014

[56] Cassidy (2014) refers to expanded US data by Piketty and Saez, showing that in 2012, the top 1% took 22.5% of total income. That year saw slow employment growth, but a boom in financial assets and real estate. He also mentions that between 2009 and 2012, 95% of the income growth accrued to the top 1% in the USA. In 2010, in the USA the richest 10% owned 70% of the wealth, while the top 1% owned 35% and the bottom half just 5%.

[57] See the discussion of the productivity of money in the later Section, The Future of Finance: What Shape or Design?

[58] Hardin (1968)

[59] Tett (2009)

[60] Tobin (1984)

[61] Stiglitz (2003: 9-11), lists the seeds of destruction as: the boom itself, leading to a classic bubble, with asset prices unrelated to underlying value; bad accounting providing bad information (in fact, even fraud as in the case of Enron and WorldCom); an outmoded regulatory system not keeping up with technology (many problems of the 1990s can be traced to deregulation in telecoms, electricity and finance); and a cut in the capital gain tax, feeding speculation – those earning money by speculation were taxed less than those who earned their keep through work.

[62] *Ibid:* xiii

[63] See *The Economist*, 'Briefing the Dodd-Frank Act: Too big not to fail', Feb. 18, 2012. While the Federal Reserve Act of 1913 comprised 29 pages, and the Banking Act, commonly known as Glass-Steagall, 32 pages, the Dodd-Frank Act, passed in July, 2010, approached 1000 pages, just for the proposed Volcker rule, which prohibits proprietary trading by banks and limits their trading activities to intermediation on behalf of clients.

[64] It is not only in the law that governmental resources are expanded to keep the financial machine in order, but also in technological investment so as to detect security manipulation. See Scannell (2014).

[65] See *The Economist*, 'More questions than answers', Dec. 24, 2013. The Volcker rule was passed on Dec. 10, 2013, and came into effect on April 1, 2014. It contains 963 pages, with 2,826 footnotes and 1,347 questions.

[66] Shiller (2012: 88) contrasts the $1.4 million per day spent in lobbying by the financial sector to the $2 million per year afforded by the Americans for Financial Reform, a lobby group representative coalition of consumer rights, civil rights, investor, retiree, community, labour, religious and certain business groups. Pressure to reverse or mitigate financial legislation persists. See Morgenson (2015).

[67] Implementation of new rules until March 31, 2018. See BIS International Regulatory Framework for Banks (Basel III) at http://bit.ly/tpMLV29 and http://bit.ly/tpMLV30

[68] With equity of $184 billion supporting total assets of $2.27 trillion at December 31, 2011 under the generally accepted accounting principles (GAAP), JP Morgan Chase's balance sheet is shown to be less of a fortress

when certain off-balance sheet items, primarily derivatives, are fully accounted for and not netted off. Total assets, after adjustment as required by the International Financial Reporting Standards (IFRS) jump to $4.06 trillion, with other debt (other than deposits and long-term debt) increasing from $698 billion under GAAP to $2.49 trillion under IFRS. See Admati & Hellwig (2013: 85). At June 30, 2013, assets were $2.4 trillion. See Admati (2013).

[69] *Ibid*: 179. See also Wolf (2013a).

[70] O'Connor, Cadman & Goff (2014)

[71] See 'Economic Inclusion and Financial Integrity – an Address to the Conference on Inclusive Capitalism', May 27, 2014. http://bit.ly/tpMLV64

[72] Wooley & Vayanos (2012) plead for large institutional investors, including sovereign wealth funds, to take the lead in adopting a long-term fundamental value approach to investment management

[73] See treatment of the contribution to the crisis by over-indebted households in Mian & Sufi (2014).

[74] Akerlof & Shiller (2009: 176)

[75] *Ibid*: 72

[76] Kay (2014)

[77] *The Economist*, 'The new age of crony capitalism', March 15, 2014

[78] See Tett (2013a)

[79] Piketty (2014) shows that the Kuznets bell-shaped curve, which assumes that wealth increases with the early stages of industrialization, but subsequently declines, is faulty.

[80] For discussion of policy instruments used by the Fed, see Wessel (2009) and Akerlof & Schiller (2009: 90-96).

[81] Reinhart & Rogoff (2009: 213)

[82] Reinhart & Rogoff (2010)

[83] See the paper by students at the University of Massachusetts, Amherst: Herndon *et al.* (2013).

[84] Tett (2013b)

[85] Turner (2013a)

[86] Turner (2014)

[87] Blyth (2013)

[88] See concern over the Bank of England's 'help-to-buy' policy and how it might be preparing the ground for another real estate bubble in Allen *et al.* (2014).

[89] *84th BIS Annual Report*, June 29, 2014. http://bit.ly/tpMLV72

[90] Giles & O'Connor (2014)

[91] Yellen (2014)

[92] White (2012)

[93] Wolf (2014c: 333)

[94] See the Conclusion of Wolf's book for his proposals.

[95] See as illustration Yellen (2014).

[96] See Wolf (2014c: 209-213), for discussion of the Chicago Plan. See also Wolf (2013b) and Turner (2013b).

[97] Wolf (2014c: 325)

[98] *Ibid*: 351

[99] Raghuram (2013)

[100] Tett (2013a)

[101] Shiller (2012: 6)

[102] Blinder (2013: 433)

Chapter 3

[1] Hawking & Mlodinow (2010: 18)

[2] For a discussion of the history of the Enlightenment, see Davies (1997).

[3] Screpanti & Zamagni (2005: 55-58)

[4] Bentham (1789/1907) saw himself as introducing new "standards of detailed accuracy comparable to those of natural sciences, new methods of enquiry and a new critical awareness of the dangers of vagueness and ambiguity and hasty generalizations" – see Introduction, p. xxxvi

[5] *Ibid.* Chapter 4. The unit of pleasure or pain is understood through its intensity, duration, certainty or uncertainty, propinquity or remoteness, fecundity, purity and extent

[6] The NOMA (non overlapping *magisteria*) principle was formulated by Richard Whately in Oxford in 1829. NOMA stipulates that economics should be separated from ethics and politics; hence the *homo oeconomicus* metaphor.

[7] Mill (1848). Later Mill was to concern himself with other human needs, as I discuss in Chapter 5.

[8] Bronk (2009: 48)

[9] Lewin (1996)

[10] *Ibid.*

[11] However, as emphasis in economics shifted from production to sales, while efficiency in production was maintained, efficiency in use has given way to maximization of sales, resulting in detrimental wastage.

[12] Philip Henry Wicksteed and Vilfredo Pareto played key roles in introducing instrumentality. In later life, Pareto gave up the study of economics for sociology, in an attempt to try to find out why his abstract mathematical theories did not work out in practice.

[13] Lewin (1996)

[14] Frank & Bernanke (2007: viii)

[15] Friedman (1953) quoted in Lewin (1996)

[16] Lewin (1996)

[17] Screpanti & Zamagni (2005)

[18] Lewin (1996)

[19] Skousen (2007: 166)

[20] *Ibid.*

[21] Because it is difficult to use underlying physical laws to predict human behaviour, effective theory is used. In physics, an effective theory is a framework created to model certain observed phenomena without describing in detail all the underlying processes. Economics is also an effective theory, based on the assumption that people are free to evaluate their alternative courses of action and choose the best.

[22] Hawking & Mlodinow (2010: 3)

[23] Smith (1776/1998)

[24] Smith (1759/1976)

[25] Skousen (2007: 29). See also Rand (1964). Rand continues to have a close following among conservatives, including Alan Greenspan, former Chairman of the Fed.

[26] O'Neill (2002)

[27] Stiglitz (2003)

[28] Albrow (2009). See also work by the anthropologist Pierre Bourdieu in this field.

[29] Havel, Vaclav, *The Art of the Impossible: Politics as Morality in Practice* (quoted in Anderson 2008).

[30] See Adam Curtis's 4-part television documentary 'Century of the Self' (2002).

[31] Dichter (1960)

[32] The advertising industry is finding it increasingly hard to maintain this 'illusion' in an age of mass scepticism. Consumers are increasingly familiar with the tricks of marketing. See Schumpeter, "We want to be your friend," *The Economist*, Feb. 1, 2014

[33] *The Economist* (Dec. 17, 2011) "Retail Therapy"

[34] Schumacher (1973) and Kumar (2012)

[35] Scruton (2000: 32)

[36] Veblen (1899/2007)

[37] (*Ibid*: 22)

[38] Scruton (2000: 62)

[39] *Ibid*: 55

[40] Gore (2013: xxvii)

[41] *Ibid*: 339

[42] 'Approaching a state shift in Earth's biosphere', *Nature* 486: 52-58, June 7, 2012

[43] Gore (2013: 143)

[44] Kennedy, Robert F. (March 18, 1968) Address at the University of Kansas on the GNP

[45] Klein (2014: 58)

[46] Bronk (2009: 48)

[47] Veblen (1932: 17)

[48] All references in these two paragraphs are from Horkheimer (1946). See in particular pp. v, 7, 30, and 104

[49] All the quotations from Jacques Ellul are from Ellul (1964). See in particular pp. xxvi, 11, 47, 55, 94, and 162

[50] This very important topic covers too vast a territory to be discussed here.

However, it impacts on many issues treated in this book and cannot be ignored. Sherry Turkle (2011), a world expert on the psychological and social effects of technology, writes: "We have invented inspiring and enhancing technologies, yet we have allowed them to diminish us". The onward advance of artificial intelligence and self-determining robots will not only affect jobs but also present a potential moral dilemma. See Technology Quarterly, *The Economist*, June 2, 2012. Recently, Stephen Hawking, Peter Thiel and Elon Musk have warned about the risk artificial intelligence poses to the human being. On Hawking, see 'Genuine concerns about artificial intelligence', *Financial Times*, Dec. 2, 2014.

[51] Rifkin (2014)

[52] A study by academics at Oxford University suggests that 47% of today's jobs could be automated in the next two decades. See 'Coming to an office near you', *The Economist* editorial, Jan. 18, 2014. Also for a discussion of how employment is being transformed, see 'Workers on tap', and 'The Future of Work', *The Economist*, Jan. 3, 2015.

[53] Lanier (2010: 6 and 19). See also 'The myth of AI: An interview with Jaron Lanier', *Edge*, Nov. 14, 2014 http://bit.ly/tpMLV96

[54] Compare this to the discussion of contemplation as enhancing knowledge in the Introduction and the call for reflection by neuroscientists in Chapter 5.

[55] Lanier (2010: 5)

[56] Bronk (2009)

[57] 'The Sign of the Times' in Carlyle (1882)

[58] *Ibid.*

[59] Mill (1848)

[60] Ruskin (1862/2010)

[61] Bronk (2009: 55)

[62] Although Mill wrote of the human pursuit of wealth as a central motivating force, he explored happiness removed from wealth. He was a thinker full of apparent contradictions. He was a Socialist, but he defended free enterprise. He believed in the merits of property in upholding liberty, but he questioned the justice of private property. (Hayek believed this kind of thinking leads to an eventual attack on private property and wealth.) He was an early feminist and argued for the rights of women in *On the Subjection of Women*. Despite writing about economic man, he longed for the bliss of a voluntary communitarian village, for a New Harmony, a United Order. See Bronk (2009: 38) and Mill (2006).

[63] Coleridge (1817)

[64] Bronk (2009: 44)

[65] Shelley, Percy B. (1821) 'A Defense of Poetry' in Duerksen (1970)

[66] Wilkinson & Pickett (2010) and (2014).

[67] Putnam (2000: 359)

[68] Stiglitz *et al.* (2009)

[69] Office of National Statistics, Measuring National Well-Being: Life in the UK 2012, Nov. 20, 2012

[70] Layard (2005: 113)

[71] Layard (2005)

[72] Stiglitz (2012) and Piketty (2014)

[73] Gilbert (2006: 219)

[74] *Ibid*: 222

[75] Study by Kahneman, Daniel and Angus Deaton, 'High income improves evaluation of life but not emotional wellbeing', *PNAS*, August 4, 2010, shows that, while emotional wellbeing rises with income, there is no further improvement beyond an income of $75,000. While low income exacerbates emotional pain and causes low life evaluation, high income buys life satisfaction, but not happiness. http://bit.ly/tpMLV82

[76] As discussed in Bok (2010: 134 and 145)

[77] Bentham (1789/1907) quoted in Kahneman (2011: 377)

[78] Layard (2005: 12)

[79] *Financial Times* (Sept. 10, 2012) 'Global economy: Not so different this time'.

[80] Screpanti & Zamagni (2005)

[81] *Ibid*: 9

[82] Fisher (1930: 501)

[83] Kahneman (2011)

[84] Turner (2010)

[85] Pope Francis, 'My message to the World Economic Forum at Davos', read by Cardinal Turkson, Jan. 21, 2014. http://bit.ly/tpMLV86

[86] Quoting from Pope Benedict XVI's *Charity in Truth*, 11.

[87] Georgescu-Roegen (1975)

[88] Saramago, José, *Canarias 7*, Interview by Esperanza Pamplona, Feb. 20, 1994

[89] Tagore (1928)

Chapter 4

[1] Hesiod, *Theogony*. This is but one of many tales in Greek myth. Contrast this with the story of the constitution of the world told by Pherecydes of Syros and recounted in Chapter 5.

[2] *The Prince* was written circa 1513, but published only in 1532.

[3] In this regard, Machiavelli was influenced by his friend, Francesco Guicciardini who wrote: "It is a law of nature, that every man minds his interest only", in *Dialogue on the Government of Florence*. Guicciardini was an important political writer of the Renaissance, who in *The History of Italy* paved the way for a new style in history, based on realistic analysis, drawing on government records as well as his own experience in politics.

[4] Bobbitt (2013: 8)

[5] Machiavelli (1517/1531/1997: xvi)

[6] Skinner (1981:40)

[7] Machiavelli (1532/1999: 65) writes that one can come to grief through ethical behaviour: "The gulf between how one should live and how one does live is so wide that a man who neglects what is actually done for what should be done moves towards self-destruction rather than self-preservation".

[8] Bobbitt (2013: Prologue)

[9] See discussion in Screpanti & Zamagni (2005: 24-25).

[10] *Discourses on Livy* was posthumously published, one year before *The Prince*, but it had been written four years later than *The Prince*.

[11] Skinner (1981: 58-61)

[12] Livy, who lived between 59 BCE and 17 CE, during the last days of the Roman republic, wrote *The Early History of Rome*.

[13] Skinner (1981: 64) writes that while the preservation of liberty is essential to greatness, the growth of corruption is fatal to liberty.

[14] References in this paragraph are to Machiavelli (1517/1531/1997) pp. x, xvi, and 68.

[15] Hobbes (1651/1997: 116): "for the atteyning of peace, and conservation of

themselves thereby, have made an Artificiall Man, which we call a Common-Wealth; so also have they made Artificial Chains, called *Civill Lawes*, which they themselves, by mutual covenants, have fastned at one end, to the lips of that Man, or Assembly, to whom they have given the Soveraigne Power."

[16] (*Ibid*: 117): "The Lawes are of no power to protect them, without a Sword in the hands of a man, or men, to cause those laws to be put in execution."

[17] "*Homo homini lupus*" – this can be contrasted with a famous quote from Genovesi: "*Homo homini natura amicus*". (Man is by nature friend to man.)

[18] Hobbes (1642/1651/2000: Dedicatory Letter)

[19] *Ibid*: viii, 1

[20] This is why Locke could not agree with Hobbes and refused to meet him, as discussed in Chapter 1.

[21] Mandeville (1714/1924). First appearing in parts in pamphlet form, it was not given much attention until an edition came out in 1723 with the poem, accompanied by a commentary *An Enquiry into the Origin of Moral Virtue*.

[22] See F.B. Kaye's Commentary in Mandeville (1714/1924: 48)

[23] Smith (1759/1976: 308-313)

[24] See Montaigne (1991) Essay 23, p. 130. Montaigne called this essay *De la coustume...* 'custom' for him has essentially the same sense as *ethos* for Aristotle, for whom this means *custom* or *habit*

[25] Livy, *The Early History of Rome*, p. 34, quoted in Machiavelli (1517/1531/1997: 13)

[26] This discussion of the self is adapted from Maritain (1946/1967).

[27] Martin Luther King, 'I Have a Dream' speech, Aug. 28, 1963.

[28] Ferry (2010) calls this the "be yourself" culture. I discuss it in Chapter 6.

[29] Aristotle (350/1908: Book 1, chapter 7)

[30] In this respect, Aristotle is similar to Confucius who believed in balance. A famous analogy by Confucius is that if a hanging pail is too full, it tips over and overflows; a pail in balance is neither empty nor too full.

[31] Sigmund (1988: 92)

[32] Skidelsky & Skidelsky (2012: 8)

[33] Keynes (1930b)

[34] Rational choice theory implies that an individual acts in balancing costs against benefits to arrive at a choice that maximizes personal advantage.

[35] Appiah (2008: 39)

[36] Putnam (2004: 75)

[37] See treatment of Aristotle in Nussbaum (2001a) Chapter 11

[38] See Appiah (2008: 172) and Nussbaum (2001a: 328)

[39] Aristotle (350/1986: 202)

[40] *Ibid*: 225

[41] MacIntyre (2006) Vol. 2, p. 4

[42] For discussion of the Dalai Lama (2013), see p. xii, xiii, and 18-19

[43] See Sen (2010) Chapter 2 for discussion of John Rawls

[44] See Sen (2010) Chapter 3 for discussion of institutions

[45] Sen (2010: 81) discusses Galbraith (1952) *American Capitalism*

[46] See earlier discussion of Machiavelli in *Discourses on Livy*, presenting a similar position.

[47] Sen (2010: 205)

[48] For a discussion of participatory democracy or the "bourgeois public sphere" of public opinion, read also Habermas (1989).

[49] Sandel (2010: 9)

[50] *Ibid:* 28

[51] All quotations here are from Pope Francis (2013: § 53 - § 85).

[52] Stiglitz (2012: xv-xvi)

[53] See reference to the power of Wall Street in influencing regulation through a provision that would roll back part of Dodd-Frank and allow banks to trade certain derivatives in Luce, Edward, 'Too big to resist: Wall Street's comeback', *Financial Times*, Dec. 14, 2014.

[54] Shaftesbury (1711: 336)

[55] Smith (1759/1976: 86)

[56] Bruni (2012b: 86)

[57] Bruni & Sugden (2008)

[58] *Ibid*: 38

[59] See Sandel (2012)

[60] *Ibid*: 13. In 2009, Sandel delivered the Reith Lectures, 'A New Citizenship', two of which were on morals and markets.

[61] Screpanti & Zamagni (2005: 23)

[62] Sartre (1946)

[63] To learn more about his thinking, see Ricoeur (1992).

Chapter 5

[1] All references in these last two paragraphs are to Wilson (2012). See in particular pp. 16, 247, 192, 197 and 241

[2] All references in these last three paragraphs are to Jackendoff (2007). See in particular pp.109, 157, 102, 145 and 161

[3] Williams (2011)

[4] Packard & Rigby (2011)

[5] Barker (2013)

[6] A golden parachute is a substantial payment upon the departure of a senior executive from a corporation; the resignation may be at the request of the Board of Directors.

[7] Shotter & Barker (2013)

[8] Schafer (2014)

[9] Veblen (1899/2007)

[10] Another name for Ge with which we are more familiar is Gaia.

[11] Kirk *et al.* (1983) and Schibli (1990)

[12] Schibli (1990: 2). A mathematician, Thales was regarded by Aristotle also as the first philosopher; he attempted to explain the nature of things without resorting to mythology.

[13] The political philosopher Antonio Maria Baggio has developed a theory of fraternity in politics and uses the tale of Pherecydes.

[14] Nussbaum (2001b: 327-335)

[15] Dalai Lama, 'Incorporating Ethics and Compassion into Business Life: A Conversation between His Holiness the Dalai Lama and Academic and Business Leaders', Santa Clara University, Feb. 24, 2014, http://bit.ly/tpMLV85

[16] Karen Armstrong (2011), a proponent of inter-religious dialogue, has proposed compassion as a guide for action.

[17] See the discussion in Mill (1865/1908).

[18] Although love is featured in the next chapter, the discussion of Comte and altruism fits in well here.

[19] Freud (1920/2003)

[20] The discovery of mirror neurons by Giacomo Rizzolatti *et al.* at the University of Parma, Italy in the 1990s helped explain why primates mimic behaviour. Further study showed the presence of mirror neurons in humans and their possible role in the development of language and understanding. For a discussion of learning through imitation as the basis of human culture, see Rizzolatti & Craighero (2004). See also de Waal & Preston (2002) for an argument that mirror neurons in humans account for empathy.

[21] While Martha Nussbaum makes a clear distinction between *empathy* and *compassion*, many use these words interchangeably.

[22] Hoffman (2000: 29)

[23] For discussion by Varela (1999), see pp. 7-19, 35, 65 and 67-69.

[24] *Ibid*: 67-69

[25] This is in agreement with Augustine's Christian teaching foundation: "know and love thyself". I discuss this in Chapter 6.

[26] Varela (1999: 71-74)

[27] Ricoeur (1992)

[28] Schopenhauer (1840/1995: Sections 17 and 18). We can compare his discussion of justice as a cardinal virtue to Aristotle's description of justice as the virtue that enables all other virtues (see Chapter 1).

[29] *Ibid*: 143. Note the similarity in approach to Paul Ricoeur's vision of the other as oneself.

[30] Schopenhauer criticized Immanuel Kant's categorical imperative and Kant's denial that moral laws are based on convention or nature. He agrees that Kant's moral imperative can be a guide for conduct, but rejects the idea that humans act only out of duty.

[31] *Ibid*: 138

[32] Likewise, the Dalai Lama refers to our *shared humanity*. He says that we all suffer and we all desire happiness. Bentham refers to the human desire to minimize pain and maximize pleasure. Today pleasure is often seen as happiness, but I discuss in this book how happiness and pleasure are distinct.

[33] See discussion of Aquinas in Pieper (1947: 39)

[34] For the discussion by Varela (1999) see pp. 26-31, 35-36 and 75.

[35] Varela (1999: 34) and Buber (1965/2002: 20)

[36] Dalai Lama (2013: 81)

[37] Darwin (1871)

[38] Rifkin (2010: 990-92)

[39] Darwin (1871)

[40] For discussion by Wilson (2012), see pp. 248, 289 and 226.

[41] For discussion by Hoffman (2000), see pp. 1, 3, 7, 9 and 149.

[42] I discussed Rawls and his theory of justice in Chapter 4.

[43] Hoffman (2000: 21)

[44] For discussion of Damasio (2010[a]), see pp. 291, 297, 292 and 24.

[45] Damasio (2010b)

[46] Ricoeur (1992)

[47] Mill (1868/2001: 31-33). See also Bruni & Sugden (2011).

[48] Martha Nussbaum refers to the central human capabilities as: life; bodily health; bodily integrity (freedom of movement and protection from assault and violence); senses, imagination and thought (enabled by education and freedom of expression); emotions (freedom from fear and anxiety); practical reason (ability to engage in critical reflection); affiliation (living freely without discrimination); nature; play; and control over one's environment (political freedom and material rights). See discussion in Nussbaum (2001b: 416-418).

[49] Dalai Lama (2013: 48)

[50] *Ibid*: 48

[51] Pieper (1947)

[52] Fuller (1981: xi)

Chapter 6

[1] Thomas Merton

[2] All definitions are from Lewis (1988). See in particular pp. 33, 57, 91 and 129.

[3] Arendt (1929/1996: 3)

[4] Marion (2003: 1)

[5] *Ibid*: 71

[6] Robertson (1954)

[7] Nieli (2006)

[8] For his research and findings, see Sorokin (1954/1982)

[9] Nieli (2006: 337)

[10] In the essay, 'What's gone wrong with democracy', *The Economist*, March 1, 2014, discusses corruption of democracy by special interests as one of its threats.

[11] Quoted by Sorokin (1954/1982: 7)

[12] *Ibid*: 484

[13] Pope Francis has fired the imagination across all segments of society, including non-Christians, through his openness, understanding, humility and compassion. During his first year, his ministry featured prominently in all major magazines and newspapers. For illustration, see his interview in *La Repubblica*, Oct. 1, 2013. http://bit.ly/tpMLV37

[14] On this and the subsequent discussion, see Sorokin (1954/1982)

[15] See Chapter 4 for discussion of Hoffman.

[16] See Sorokin for case studies of how people came to the discovery of love, particularly Chapter 8, 9 and 12. Both the Dalai Lama and Schopenhauer talk of compassion stirred by the observation of suffering.

[17] Freud (1934)

[18] All references in these paragraphs are to Ferry (2010). See in particular pp. 215, 424, 264 and 266.

[19] Ferry refers to this as the history of the *bohème*, beginning in the mid-19th century and coming to fruition in the 1960s – see Chapter 1 of his book.

[20] Descartes' declaration "I think, therefore I am" set the foundation for Enlightenment thinking, based purely on reason.

[21] Aristotle (350/1986: 31)

[22] Lewis (1966)

[23] Integral theory seeks to integrate knowledge from disparate fields, in order to arrive at a holistic understanding.

[24] The neurologist and psychiatrist and Holocaust survivor Viktor Frankl (1959-2004) writes that "striving to find a meaning in one's life is the primary motivational force in man". He also writes: "the more one forgets himself – by giving himself to a cause to serve or another person to love – the more human he is and the more he actualizes himself". And he acknowledges the role of suffering in human transformation: "the uniquely human potential at its best, which is to transform a personal tragedy into a triumph, to turn one's predicament into a human achievement".

[25] Bronk (2009: 38) and Mill (2006)

[26] In his *Autobiography* (Mill 2006), Chapters 6 and 7, Mill describes his relationship with Harriet Taylor and her influence on his work.

[27] Mill (2006: 193)

[28] In a draft of his *Autobiography* (Mill 2006: 113), Mill had notated but then cancelled: "in our schemes for improving human affairs we overlooked human beings".

[29] Although *The Subjection of Women* was written after the death of his wife, he attributes the "most profound and striking passages" to her, as the result of "innumerable conversations and discussions". See Mill (2006: 265)

[30] Bruni (2006: 98)

[31] Martin Luther King was a student of Paul Tillich and did his doctoral thesis on his writings. This perspective was developed by Tillich, as I shall discuss.

[32] This agrees with Sorokin's treatment of love and the idealistic culture, infusing the spiritual and intuitive into the material, thus enabling a balanced picture of reality. See King (1967).

[33] Discussion in this section is drawn from Tillich (1960). See specifically pp. 26, 45 and 22.

[34] Hanh (1993)

[35] Hanh (2003)

[36] See Augustine (417: VIII, 8, 12)

[37] Coda (2010) and (2008).

[38] Pope Francis is taking up the example of St. Francis of Assisi.

[39] Francis of Assisi, *Canticle of the Sun*

[40] Teilhard de Chardin (1959/2004) and (1959/2002).

[41] We can compare this to Sorokin's cultural progression from the *material* or *sensate* to the *spiritual* or *ideational*. See also 'Supreme Love and the Supraconscious', in Sorokin (1954/1982) Chapter 8.

[42] St. Paul, Colossians 2:9

[43] Cheng (2009). Compare Cheng's treatment to Sorokin's discussion of the transcendence reached by great musicians.

[44] Based on extensive research into artistic expression, Sorokin and his team discovered that the classical music masters, such as Bach, Handel,

Mozart and Beethoven, moved between the elevated heights of this world and the transcendental. See Nieli (2006) p. 65.

[45] Cheng (2009) pp. 58-72

[46] 'Ode to A Grecian Urn'

[47] Dostoyevsky, *The Idiot*, Part III, Chapter 1

[48] "Oh beauty, belatedly I loved you, so old and yet so new! Belatedly I loved you! I sought you without, while you were within." Augustine (401: X, 27).

[49] Augustine, *Sermon*, 34, 2, quoted in Arendt (1929/1996: 77).

[50] Hitchens (2005)

[51] Frankfurt (2004)

[52] Boltanski (1990) p. 239

[53] Quoted by Sorokin (1954/1982) p. 459

[54] *Ibid*, Chapter 23

[55] "And because they were lonely and perplexed, because they had all come from a place of sadness and worry and defeat, and because they were all going to a new mysterious place, they huddled together; they talked together; they shared their lives, their food, and the things they hoped for in the new country...In the evening a strange thing happened: the twenty families became one family; the children were the children of all. The loss of home became one loss, and the golden time in the West was one dream....In the evening, sitting about the fires, the twenty were one." Steinbeck (1939/1988: 139-140).

[56] See Nussbaum (2013c) Chapter 2 for her discussion of love versus competition in Mozart's opera 'The Marriage of Figaro'.

Integration

[1] See 'Hayek on Moral Values and Altruism' at http://bit.ly/tpMLV84

[2] Highlighted by Mark Carney (2014).

[3] The March 31, 2014 report by the Intergovernmental Panel on Climate Change (IPCC) paints a dire picture, affecting ecosystems, human health, food and water security, and which requires action without delay; however, consensus remains elusive. See Yokohama, 'In the balance', *The Economist*, April 5, 2014

[4] Keynes (1936: 162)

[5] Contrary to Thomas Hobbes, Rawls presupposes the human propensity for good.

[6] For Martha Nussbaum, and in line with the understanding of ***humanism*** in this book, it does not imply anti-religious sentiment, contrary to the way it is understood by some. See Nussbaum (2013b).

[7] Carney (2014)

[8] Beinhocker & Hanauer (2014)

[9] For a discussion of how the investment community views sustainability, see Melo Antunes (2007) – the author's married name.

[10] Students are calling for a revised curriculum that has to do with the needs of the world. On Nov. 2, 2011, a group of students at Harvard walked out of Economics 10, in protest against the bias inherent in the introductory economics class, "a course that espouses a specific—and limited—view of economics that we believe perpetuates problematic and inefficient systems of economic inequality in our society today," and to join a march in solidarity with the Occupy movement. See 'An Open Letter to Greg Mankiw', *Harvard Political Review*, Nov. 2, 2011 – http://bit.ly/tpMLV77. Student action in this regard has expanded, but academic resistance persists. See also the BBC Radio 4 podcast, 'Teaching Economics after the Crash' http://bit.ly/tpMLV88.

[11] For a new approach to economics, see Chang (2014).

[12] Quoted by Adair Turner (2010).

[13] See for example the Principles for Responsible Investment, under the aegis of the United Nations; this initiative has now 1350 signatories. http://bit.ly/tpMLV78

[14] Woolley (2013)

[15] Minsky (2008)

[16] See 'Financial-technology firms: Revenge of the nerds', *The Economist*, Aug. 3, 2013. Also 'Lending clubs surge 56% on launch,' *Financial Times*, Dec. 11, 2014

[17] Waters (2014)

[18] Schumacher (1973)

[19] See Schumacher (1977) p. 145 and Chapter 10. He writes on p. 141: "How is it that liberty and equality cease to be mutually antagonistic and become 'reconciled' when brotherliness is present?".

[20] Barber (2012)

[21] Giddens (1991).

Index

L

M

N

O

P

Q

R

S

T

V

W

Y

Z

International Futures Forum

International Futures Forum (IFF) is a non-profit organisation established to support a transformative response to complex and confounding challenges and to restore the capacity for effective action in today's powerful times.

At the heart of IFF is a deeply informed inter-disciplinary and international network of individuals from a range of backgrounds covering a wide range of diverse perspectives, countries and disciplines. The group meets as a learning community as often as possible, including in plenary session. And it seeks to apply its learning in practice. IFF takes on complex, messy, seemingly intractable issues – notably in the arenas of health, learning, governance and enterprise – where paradox, ambiguity and complexity characterise the landscape, where rapid change means yesterday's solution no longer works, where long-term needs require a long-term logic and where only genuine innovation has any chance of success.

www.internationalfuturesforum.com

Triarchy Press

Triarchy Press is an independent publisher of new alternative thinking (altThink) about organisations and society, and practical ways to apply that thinking. In our partnership with IFF we are lucky to work with some of the most inspiring thinkers and practitioners in the field. They challenge us to embrace the potential of change rather than retreat into the familiar – revealing wiser ways of preparing for an uncertain future.

Other IFF titles include: *Humanising Healthcare, Three Horizons, Dancing at the Edge, Ten Things to do in a Conceptual Emergency, Ready for Anything, Economies of Life, Beyond Survival: A Short Course in Pioneering* and *Transformative Innovation in Education (2nd Edition).*

www.triarchypress.net

CPSIA information can be obtained
at www.ICGtesting.com
Printed in the USA
LVHW020906070821
694475LV00006B/123

9 781909 470606